Sleep Well
Lead Well

(With AEI∞ Model of Supreme Leadership)

YATIN J. PATEL

MD, MBA, FCCP

Profits from the sale of this book and from my consulting work support a global initiative, F.E.M.A.L.E. (Food, Education, Medicines, And Love for Everyone) Ashram, aimed at changing the world by educating one neuron at a time through innovative intervention using the Internet and other media.

Father Ted Hesburgh (left), whose inspiration and
blessings made this book possible

To my wife, Dipti, for bringing love into my life
To my children, Priyata, Pooja, and Parth, for bringing joy into my life
To my dad, for the gift of the written word
To my mom, for those sleepless nights when my asthma acted up

Acknowledgments

I am eternally grateful to the following thought leaders and researchers whose lifetime of dedication made this work possible:

Jessica Payne, PhD, University of Notre Dame, Notre Dame, IN

Ralph Downey III, PhD, Loma Linda University, Loma Linda, CA

Matthew P. Walker, PhD, University of California, Berkley, CA

E. Van der Helm, PhD, and N. Gujar, PhD, University of California, Berkeley, CA

Thomas Roth, PhD, Henry Ford Medical Center, Detroit, MI

William Dement, MD, PhD, and Christian Guilleminault, MD, Stanford University, Stanford, CA

Teofilo L. Lee-Chiong Jr., MD, National Jewish Medical Center, Denver, CO

Thomas J. Balkin, PhD, Walter Reed Army Institute of Research, Bethesda, MD

Nancy J. Wesensten, MD, Walter Reed Army Institute of Research, Bethesda, MD

Sara C. Mednick, MD, University of California, San Diego, CA

Robert Stickgold, MD, Harvard Medical School, Boston, MA

Charles A. Czeisler, MD, PhD, Harvard Medical School, Boston, MA

Diedre Barrett, PhD, Harvard Medical School, Boston, MA

Daniel Goleman, PhD, researcher and author of *Emotional Intelligence*

Matthew A. Wilson, PhD, Massachusetts Institute of Technology, Cambridge, MA

Special thanks to my gurus at Mendoza College of Business, Notre Dame University, for their guidance and encouragement:

Leo Burke, director, Executive Integral Leadership

Joseph Holt, director, Executive Ethics Program

James H. Davis, PhD, professor, Family Business

William P. Sexton, PhD, Executive Leadership

Sarv Devaraj, associate professor, Management

I am grateful for the help provided by the following friends: Jill Bodensteiner, Jeff Nelson, Thomas Brown, Deb and Paul Cafiero, Tom Karnowski, and Kevin Patel.

The U.S. space shuttle *Challenger* exploded on January 28, 1986, seventy-three seconds into its tenth flight, killing all seven crewmembers, including a civilian schoolteacher, Christa McAuliffe. From an engineering standpoint, the disaster was caused by the failure of an "O" ring in one of the solid rocket boosters to properly seat on ignition. The "O" ring lost flexibility because of the cold temperatures on the day of the launch. The failure to accurately evaluate the reliability of the "O" rings under prevailing weather conditions has been attributed to insufficient sleep on the part of NASA managers involved in the launch decision. Of the three high-level NASA managers involved, two had had less than three hours of sleep for three consecutive nights prior to the launch.

The Role of Sleep in Sustaining Individual and Organizational Effectiveness

Nancy J. Wesensten, Thomas J. Balkin, and Gregory Belenky

Preface

The human race imposes a tremendous burden on its leaders. This burden gets worse during a catastrophe or a huge opportunity. During these times, our leaders' sleep deprivation gets worse, and their sleep debt continues to mount. As a result, because of sleep debt's deleterious effect on their executive function, our leaders are only a shadow of what they really can be—at the very time they need to be at their best.

Research on sleep deprivation's effect on executive function was in its infancy when we founded the Center for Sleep Studies and started our pulmonary and sleep-medicine practice in 1994. In last ten years though, thanks to excellent work by leading sleep researchers around the world, an explosion of discoveries has proven the deleterious effects of sleep deprivation on emotional intelligence, informational intelligence, and, therefore, executive function. Studies have further shown that even the strongest motivation cannot reverse these deleterious effects.

Studies of the brain using positron-emission tomography (PET) and functional magnetic resonance imaging (MRI) have shown severely reduced function in sleep-deprived humans in the prefrontal cortex (the executive center), which, among other things, is responsible for planning, creative problem solving, information processing, decision making, and effective communication. The prefrontal cortex is also responsible for accurate self-assessment, which unfortunately makes us unaware of this severe handicap. To make matters worse, the amygdala (the fear center) shows increased activity, which puts the leader in fight-or-flight mode, as opposed to collaborate-and-create mode. Sleep deprivation also leads to lower goal setting, because of a heightened fear of failure. If you add to this mix a tiny structure located at the base of the cerebral cortex (suprachiasmatic nucleus), you have severely suboptimal leadership at its best and disastrous leadership at its worst. The suprachiasmatic nucleus—the circadian pacemaker—makes us sleepy at night and, unfortunately, in the afternoon as well. This afternoon sleepiness gets worse with mounting sleep debt, further affecting our leadership function.

Now the billion-dollar question is, "How many O-rings do sleep-deprived leaders in boardrooms across the globe overlook during key strategic decisions, mergers and acquisitions, key hiring decisions, and protracted negotiations?" And leadership is not just about avoiding errors. What about creating breakthrough products, designing disruptive innovation, creating new markets, designing and implementing a super-efficient supply chain, finding creative ways to save the environment, or using microfinancing to eliminate world poverty?

During my Executive MBA program at Notre Dame, I had the good fortune of spending several years with executives from around the world. They were CEOs, vice-presidents, senior vice-presidents, and department heads working for various multinational corporations. They were entrepreneurs, attorneys, accountants, consultants, IT experts, and a handful of doctors. They all were hardworking, dedicated, focused, and disciplined overachievers.

Jim, a road warrior in his early forties, looked over Coca Cola's sales and distribution in thirteen states in the Midwest United States. Denise, despite managing a big family, had climbed the corporate hierarchy and was now chief information officer (CIO) at an auto-manufacturing company. Steve, a consultant with Fortune 500 companies, had built a successful seven-figure annual income despite working on severely insufficient sleep while traveling from Seattle to South Bend every week. Todd, a lieutenant in the United States Navy, was standing guard in a nuclear submarine when those planes hit the World Trade Center towers on that fateful day, September 11, 2001. He had slept four hours a day for several weeks in a row. Chuck, an always-happy forty-year-old senior accountant at Ernst and Young, was leading a team of eighty professionals in thirty-five countries, even while doing an MBA at Notre Dame. Jon, the father of two young children and a regional sales manager at a multinational corporation, successfully managed a fifty-million-dollar sales budget while juggling MBA assignments and family responsibilities.

To my surprise, most, if not all, were sleep deprived even though they had achieved so much already in their careers. Yet I believed, based on extensive medical research, that they could achieve even more and ultimately reach their true God-given potential if they managed their alertness better. They could eliminate the inconsistency in their performance and further enhance their creativity. They could improve their empathy, interpersonal skills, greed for greater good, and ability to manage complex information.

> Life is so precious. Why waste
> one-third of it sleeping?

From time to time, between the Executive MBA classes, while taking a break from assignments or over a beer at Legends on the Notre Dame campus, I would hesitantly share sleep research with them and receive the following remarks:

"Yatin, I have so much going on all the time. I really don't have time for seven to eight hours of sleep. There is just not enough time in the day for me to get stuff done."

"Yatin, you have no idea how much responsibility I shoulder."

"I have achieved so much despite insufficient sleep that I think I'm immune to the effects of sleep deprivation."

"There is so much at stake that I can easily motivate myself to excel despite sleep deprivation."

"I have achieved so much by ignoring sleep. Why can't I continue to do just that?"

I would challenge them: Can you achieve more? Can alertness management help you maximize your emotional intelligence? Can it help you manage information better? Can sleep help you maximize executive output, both quantitatively and, more importantly, qualitatively?

I would probe further. What makes your executive output inconsistent despite the same ability, same expertise, and same brain? Is this inconsistency merely a result of probability distribution or macroeconomic factors? Can fluctuating alertness, with its effect on emotional intelligence and informational intelligence, cause this inconsistency? Can you leverage sleep to maximize your executive excellence through optimal emotional intelligence and informational intelligence? Can you be in the zone all the time?

Yes, you can through the AEImax model of consistent excellence. This simple model first helps you achieve rectangular alertness[1] even when running on insufficient sleep, and then teaches you to leverage this rectan-

---

1 Maximal alertness that can last sixteen hours a day

gular alertness to maximize your emotional intelligence[2] and your informational intelligence[3] to achieve consistent excellence.

Once you have ensured consistency in your performance, can you take leadership to new heights by embarking on a quest for greater good and selfless service? Can you tap into enormous and unused spiritual power to maximize your God-given potential? **Yes, you can through the AEI∞ model of supreme leadership.**

Once you start your journey toward AEI∞, how can you monitor your own performance the way you monitor your company's cash flow, stock prices, market share, and other vital parameters? This is where an intuitive, easy-to-use, and visual dashboard—the **AEI dashboard**—comes into play. The AEI dashboard provides you with real-time feedback about your leadership ability at every moment, so you avoid task-ability mismatch, manage your ability to meet the challenges of your career, and continue your journey toward AEI∞.

In the following pages, I will try to convince you to guard your sleep, both in duration and in quality, with the same tenacity you use to guard your bottom line. Both are intricately tied together. As a pulmonary physician covering intensive-care units for fifteen years, I know that sleep deprivation is sometimes unavoidable. During periods of great opportunity or unexpected calamity, sleep deprivation is unavoidable, yet leadership must be at its best. So I also devote a significant portion of this book to the task of leading well despite sleep deprivation.

This book is divided into the following five sections:

---

2 Ability to manage our own and others' emotions, ability to form social connections
3 Ability to receive, distill, digest, retain, apply, and reproduce information in an easy-to-understand manner

Section I:

- Describes the tremendous financial impact of sleep deprivation at a national level
- Describes sleep physiology, including various sleep stages, their functions, and, most interestingly, rapid eye movement (REM) sleep, its immense creative power, and how to tap into that creative power and achieve out-of-the-world thinking
- Describes good sleep habits that will give you the most restorative sleep and earn you the most return on your investment in sleep
- Helps you achieve rectangular alertness—maximal alertness that can last all day long
- Tries to settle the age-old debate about how much sleep is enough
- Describes the positive effect of regular exercise on sleep quality, alertness, emotional intelligence, informational intelligence, and, hence, leadership performance
- Discusses time-management techniques that will help you achieve sufficient sleep despite a demanding work schedule
- Teaches Patel's Relaxed Eye Muscles (PREM) nap, a revolutionary power-nap technique that can restore executive excellence despite sleep debt

Section II:

- Focuses on sleep debt and its ill effects on alertness, emotional intelligence, informational intelligence, and, thereby, executive performance
- Describes signs, symptoms, and treatments of obstructive sleep apnea, various types of insomnia, and other common sleep disorders found in corporate athletes

Section III:

- Gives you the Leader's Alertness Maximization Plan (LAMP), which will help you achieve maximal alertness despite sleep deprivation
- Provides a cure for sleep debt's ill effects on emotional intelligence and teaches simple countermeasures to eliminate those effects
- Describes deficits in informational intelligence and gives countermeasures to fight this detrimental effect
- Provides the framework for rational decision making even when sleep deprived

Section IV:

- Incorporates all we have learned into the AEI model of consistent excellence
- Teaches how to leverage alertness to achieve maximal emotional intelligence and informational intelligence, and to reach AEImax, a state of consistent excellence
- Takes the concept even further by adding selflessness and spiritual force to achieve AEI∞
- Provides a very simple, yet profoundly useful AEI dashboard, which empowers you to measure and manage your leadership performance in real time every single moment

Section V:

- Deals with several specific scenarios commonly encountered in corporate America today, and offers practical solutions specific to them
- Dedicates "Going to War When Tired" to excelling and winning tough and protracted negotiations despite insufficient sleep
- Systematically guides you to consistent excellence despite jet-lag syndrome

- Discusses the unique sleep needs of female leaders and helps them excel despite sleep problems encountered during menstruation, premenstrual syndrome, pregnancy, and menopause
- Describes our public education campaign aimed at eliminating fatalities associated with drowsy driving
- Provides simple tips on how sleep-deprived leaders can prevent injuries and fatalities resulting from drowsy driving
- Discusses challenges faced by journalists, and offers a few tips to help them excel despite their challenging work schedule

Sleep-deprived leaders have shaped the history of human civilization. Starting tonight, let us change that.

SECTION I:

Dealing with Inadequate Sleep

- ✓ Sleep? Who Cares!
- ✓ Our Leaders Get Insufficient—and Poor Quality—Sleep
- ✓ To Be an Effective Leader, You Must Embrace Change in Your Sleeping Habits
- ✓ Normal Sleep
- ✓ Invest in Sleep Hygiene and Maximize Your Return
- ✓ How Much Sleep Do We Need?
- ✓ Procrastination: The Eternal Enemy of Sufficient Sleep
- ✓ Good Time Management Will Give You Sufficient Sleep
- ✓ Discipline Will Result in Deep Sleep
- ✓ Exercise Improves Deep Sleep and Executive Output
- ✓ Prayer, Positive Emotions, and REM Sleep
- ✓ Power Nap: Your Best Investment Ever

Sleep? Who Cares!

Americans live in a culture of inadequate sleep. According to the National Sleep Foundation, Americans are some of the most sleep-deprived people on earth; 40 percent claim to get less than seven hours of sleep per night, and 75 percent maintain that, one or more nights per week, troubling sleep disorders affect their ability to get the sleep they need. Our business and political leaders get even less sleep chronically, so they carry a greater burden of sleep debt than the general population. This sleep debt gets worse during major macroeconomic events (financial-market crashes, oil spills, or erupting volcanoes) and major internal events (mergers and acquisitions, important board meetings, protracted negotiations, transcontinental sales trips, tax seasons, new product launches, or corporate restructuring).

Accumulating Sleep Debt

Most leaders approach sleep with a take-it-or-leave-it attitude, but sleep is not optional. The human body requires sleep in order to survive and operate at maximum efficiency. While the amount of sleep one requires varies somewhat from individual to individual, the average person requires between seven and eight hours of quality sleep each day. So what happens when we fail to get enough sleep? According to "The Role of Sleep in Sustaining Individual and Organizational Effectiveness" by Nancy J. Wesensten, Thomas J. Balkin, and Gregory Belenky:

> Results of brain imaging (positron-emission tomography, or PET) studies during sleep deprivation have revealed that sleep deprivation decreases brain activation. More critical is that activation is most decreased in specific brain areas—those mediating the ability to maintain alertness and vigilance and those mediating higher-order mental operations such as situational awareness, adaptability, mental agility,

judgment, initiative, anticipation, and planning. These qualities are crucial for organizational effectiveness.

Sleep deprivation will cause you to feel irritable and experience mood swings. You will experience more emotional problems, including depression or anxiety. You will have reduced ability to deal with stress. You will have impaired self-assessment and regulation. You will forget important information. You will show poor judgment, poor concentration, and an inability to make decisions. Overall, intellectual performance will decrease; critical thinking will plummet. You will increase your risk of obesity, heart disease, and even diabetes.

Additionally, your life will be shortened. It is a statistical reality that death from all causes is lowest among adults who get the required number of sleep hours per night. The death rate is significantly higher among those who sleep less than seven hours.

Your immune system will become impaired. At the University of Chicago, sleep researcher Eve van Cauter gave flu vaccine to subjects who had slept only four hours per night for the previous six nights. Their immune systems produced only half the normal number of antibodies in response. Their heart rates and blood pressure were elevated. They developed insulin resistance, and the secretion of leptin, a hormone that inhibits appetite, was reduced, making the individual more apt to gain weight.

Typically, a leader's career spans five to six decades.
And in order to provide consistent excellence that can be
sustained throughout the long career, seven to eight hours
of quality sleep per night is a must.

Tiredness at Work Can Be Hazardous to Your Health (and Costly to Your Wallet)

Historically, there are many examples of how disastrous tiredness-related accidents can be. Some of these accidents have even put humanity in danger. Well-known examples include the nuclear accidents at Chernobyl and Three Mile Island.

According to the National Sleep Foundation, workplace tiredness costs the United States at least a hundred billion dollars every year. A study published in 2005 estimated the cost of workplace sleepiness in Australia at almost 1 percent of Gross Domestic Product. Interestingly, these estimates do not include the massive cost of suboptimal leadership due to impaired decision-making, poor problem-solving, unsatisfactory communication, truncated goal-setting, inability to handle an emergency adequately, and missed opportunity for growth.

Executives who regularly travel across time zones are severely deprived of deep sleep, so they are at greater risk for suboptimal leadership, as are those who sleep less than seven hours per night.

Managers, doctors, nurses, and others working night shifts are more prone to errors or accidents because of tiredness. It has been estimated that workers' tiredness is the main and immediate cause for 18 percent of accidents and injuries occurring in the workplace. Lack of sleep is among the most frequent causes of tiredness, which impairs concentration, attentiveness, and memory. In the workplace, Lack of sleep is causing a huge burden in terms of human cost, as well as loss of efficiency, productivity, and profitability.

Overtired leaders often take small snoozes without even realizing it. Imagine taking a small snooze when driving or operating dangerous equipment. A large accumulated sleep debt makes you a danger to yourself and others.

Falling asleep at the wheel is a major cause of highway fatalities. Fatigue and driving an automobile are a dangerous combination. If you add even a small amount of alcohol to that mixture, the risk often turns deadly.

The problem is not limited to automobile operators. Notice how often operator fatigue is mentioned in reports of accidents involving other kinds of activity. Fatigue was the primary cause of one of the most devastating environmental disasters ever to occur at sea, when the *Exxon Valdez* struck Bligh Reef and spilled more than eleven million gallons of crude oil into Prince William Sound. Fatigue is also cited as a primary factor in numerous aviation accidents, and is a continuing problem for pilots and crews flying aircraft of all sizes. Pilot error involving impaired judgment and decision-making is often just a symptom of fatigue.

Fatigue was also a factor in the radiation release at Three Mile Island when shift workers failed to recognize that a main valve had broken, causing the loss of a major coolant that ultimately led to the overheating of the radioactive core. Likewise, worker fatigue was cited as a contributing cause of the methyl isocyanate release at a chemical facility in Bhopal, India.

The Huge Economic Impact of Sleep Deprivation

While the exact economic consequences of sleep deprivation in America are unknown, they are estimated to be, as discussed above, at least one hundred billion dollars per year due to lost productivity, medical expenses, sick leave, and property and environmental damage. The staggering cost of sleep deprivation also includes such tragedies as oil spills, plane crashes, and automobile accidents where lack of sleep was a factor. Additionally, less-visible costs are associated with mortality, morbidity, poor performance, other forms of accidents and injuries, quality of life, family well-being, and health care utilization.

Leaving the Brain on the Pillow

"Presenteeism" is the problem of being at work but not fully functioning. One of the chief causes of presenteeism is lack of sleep. Employees whose bodies arrive at work, but whose brains remain on a pillow at home, are commonplace in today's business environment. And it affects people of all ages. Have you ever worked in a place that seemed to be filled with zombies in the early afternoon? If you combine these individuals with those who go to work despite being ill or who suffer a chronic medical condition that prevents them from fully functioning, the problem of presenteeism becomes a phenomenon that costs American companies more than a hundred fifty billion dollars a year, exceeding even the cost of absenteeism.

In 2008, the National Sleep Foundation surveyed a thousand workers, with startling and alarming results:

- 36 percent admitted to having nodded off or fallen asleep while driving.
- 29 percent said they had fallen asleep or become very sleepy at work.
- 12 percent confessed to researchers that they had been late to work because of sleepiness.

Our Leaders Get Insufficient— and Poor Quality—Sleep

The problem of sleep deprivation is especially alarming for those in leadership positions. Studies show that these individuals sleep less and, at the same time, work harder and longer, a disturbing trend that has consequences for their health and mood. Subordinates and peers often characterize sleep-deprived leaders as grumpy, moody, miserable, and not much fun to be around.

Sleep researchers Sylvia Ann-Hewlett and Carolyn Luce discovered that:

- 62 percent of high-earning individuals work more than fifty hours per week.
- 35 percent work more than sixty hours per week.
- 10 percent work more than eighty hours a week.

These disturbing findings imply that more than 70 percent of professionals are not getting enough sleep. Consider how sleep deprivation affects those in leadership roles. Think about overtired CEOs, presidents and vice-presidents of large organizations, business owners, doctors, nurses, military personnel, nuclear-plant workers, air-traffic controllers, police and fire personnel, political leaders, and other people whose fatigue-driven mistakes have the potential to do significant harm. Should they suddenly find themselves in an emergency situation where sound judgment and the ability to make critical decisions quickly are vital, what then?

With e-mail coming on the scene over fifteen years ago, workers at all levels now find themselves stressed to the max while trying to keep up with the extra workload that e-mail brings into their daily schedule. Factoring in smartphones and other electronic gadgets that are supposed to make life easier on everyone, we now have a population that is losing valuable sleep as it tries to keep up with a growing list of responsibilities. By investing in a few more hours of sleep a night, you can improve your executive function remarkably and may extend your career by a couple of decades.

Business Leaders Talk about Sleep

Thankfully, some leaders understand the need for seven to eight hours of sleep each night. Bill Gates says he gets at least seven hours of sleep a night because "that's what I need to stay sharp and creative and upbeat." Jack Welch, according to reports from those who know him well, also needed seven hours of sleep per night when he was CEO of General Electric. Jeff Bezos, CEO of Amazon.com, sleeps eight hours a night. He says, "I'm more alert, and I think more clearly. I just feel so much better all day long if I've had eight hours." Michael Bonsignore, chairman and CEO of Honeywell International Inc., gets seven hours of sleep and claims it's a "necessary evil." Marc Andersen, co-founder of Netscape, admits to needing eight hours. He says, "I can get by on seven and a half hours without much trouble. Seven, and I start to degrade. Six is suboptimal. Five is a big problem. Four means I am a zombie."

Bill Clinton on Sleep Deprivation

In September 2007, former President Bill Clinton appeared on *The Daily Show* and talked about the current harsh relationship between the Democratic and Republican parties. He argued that sleep loss among members of Congress might be a significant contributing factor to the incivility that exists in Washington, DC. Clinton said the job of the modern-day member of Congress has significantly changed over the past thirty years, primarily because of the ongoing need to raise money. He said it is not unusual for members of Congress to travel home every weekend to attend fund-raisers. As a result, many suffer from chronic fatigue.

"I know this is an unusual theory, but I do believe sleep deprivation has a lot to do with some of the edginess of Washington today," said Clinton. "You have no idea how many Republican and Democratic members of the House and Senate are chronically sleep deprived because of this (fund-raising) system."

Leadership Crisis

An interesting phenomenon takes place when sleep deprivation occurs. The brain works harder but accomplishes less. Using real-time, state-of-the-art imaging, scientists have discovered that sleep deprivation has significant effects on how the brain functions.

For example, researchers found that, while certain parts of the brains of sleep-deprived patients remained active, one part of the brain (the language center) shuts down completely. Sleep-deprived subjects showed significantly increased activity in the amygdala, the part of the brain that signals the body to be on alert to protect itself and control emotions. Simultaneously, activity lowered significantly in the prefrontal cortex, the part of the brain that controls reasoning. Rested subjects who had received a full night's sleep had normal brain activity.

This study clearly shows that sleep-deprived people are likely to overreact to emotional challenges they would otherwise be able to negotiate without difficulty. This can lead to all sorts of interpersonal problems for average Americans, but it can spell disaster for those in leadership positions. Sleep-deprived leaders who lack emotional intelligence are a time bomb just waiting to explode. And the damages caused when this kind of explosion occurs are often severe and permanent.

> Abnormal amount of executive output is unsustainable.

Sleeplessness: A Badge of Honor

We have all heard stories about famous people who supposedly require very little sleep. Bill Clinton, Martha Stewart, Condoleezza Rice, and countless others are portrayed as special kinds of people who require only a few hours of sleep each night. As a result, many people believe that needing little sleep is a big plus. Yet, studies have shown that these short-sleepers have abnormal daytime sleepiness and that most people need at least seven hours of sleep per night for optimum biological and psychological health. There is an obvious disconnect between science and popular culture.

A study by Dr. Yvonne Harrison, a researcher at Loughborough University, Leicestershire, U.K. has shown that reducing sleep duration to less than eight hours for fourteen days causes a dose-dependent decline in neurobehavioral and cognitive function. In other words, sleeping less results in increased executive output quantitatively at the expense of quality.

Dr. Eve VanCauter, a sleep researcher and professor of medicine at the University of Chicago, says that many people today, especially in the United States, pride themselves on not getting enough sleep. "Sleeping as little as possible is viewed as a badge of honor here."

The idea that successful people do not need much sleep is an American myth that is alive and well. So, too, is the belief that the pace of life in the twenty-first century is so fast that sleep has become a luxury we often must sacrifice for the good of our careers.

Dr. VanCauter believes our society is now where we were with cigarette smoking twenty years ago. Twenty years from now, she says, research, public knowledge, and even litigation in which sleep deprivation is determined to be a basis for negligence, will combine to cause a change in public perception. She believes people will ultimately understand that sleep deprivation is dangerous—not something to be proud of.

To Be an Effective Leader, You Must Embrace Change in Your Sleeping Habits

In today's turbulent business world, where companies are dismantling bureaucratic hierarchies to become leaner organizations, and employees are expected to do more with less, many managers and executives feel abandoned. They may feel as if they are getting lost in the shuffle, or that the organization's leadership is in question. But often, those leaders are simply sleep deprived. When that happens, chaos is sure to result.

It is never too late. Change can happen, and your quest for excellence in leadership will take you places you never dreamed possible. No matter what level of management you find yourself in at the present, you can make a difference in the life of any company or corporation, large or small. But it is essential that you recognize the importance of sleep.

The world of work is different today than it was even a few decades ago. But leaders still struggle to overthrow the weight of the past. In the days of our fathers and grandfathers, rigid bureaucratic discipline dominated the lives and careers of every executive. The price of success was blind obedience.

These days, it takes a new brand of leadership to make things happen. Clarity and understanding must now replace the foggy mind-set of past years. Achieving the results you desire as a leader in the twenty-first century may seem like an uphill battle, but you can go the distance. You can come out on top as a winner. In other words, you can be a leader of tomorrow in today's world. But it can only be possible if you are thinking and making decisions with a clear head—which you will have after a good night's sleep.

Great leaders anticipate what will be needed and take action. They are not afraid to make decisions, and they know how to surround themselves with loyal and motivated workers. Don't be afraid to become the great leader that is hiding inside of you. Walt Disney said it best: "If you can dream it, you can do it!" So start dreaming of taking the first step on your leadership journey, and do so by getting enough sleep.

Sound Sleep Improves Emotional Intelligence

Many of today's true leaders use their intellect and intuition to deal with the day-to-day operations of their companies. They use their well-developed listening skills and pay strict attention to other clues, such as body language, to see and hear all the unspoken expressions of their work team members or their senior managers.

Emotional intelligence surfaced a few years back through a book published by Daniel Goleman in 1995. By definition, emotional intelligence is "a skill set or the ability to recognize, understand, and effectively cope with the demands of the workforce and the entire work environment successfully." To understand the importance of emotional intelligence and leadership, you must first understand the importance of getting a good night's sleep.

Leadership is not about how smart you are; it's what you do with what you have that counts. To become an effective leader in today's workplace, you must balance your emotional skills and leadership skills. You must become an expert in many skills, including time management, and you must factor in enough time for proper rest at night.

If you are being demanding and coercive—that is, a tyrant—you are not leading your people. You are bullying people, and they will not respect you. Nor will they respond to you as positively as you would like them to. Medical researchers have found that angry leaders are more likely than anyone else to be sleep deprived . True leaders will use all their tools and emotional intelligence to successfully inspire, motivate, listen to, and provide effective feedback to their team members to assist them in attaining their goals.

Listed below are a few important aspects of emotional intelligence. Examine how your leadership skill set incorporates them.

- *Self-awareness* means you are in touch with your emotional states as you express your feelings to others.
- *Self-regulation* means you accept responsibility for your emotional responses and learn to better manage your emotional triggers.
- *Self-motivation* means you strive to be in the moment with all work tasks and resist self-defeating thoughts when setbacks occur.
- *Empathy* means you see the world through the eyes of others.
- *Effective relationships* mean you use emotional intelligence to influence and persuade others and build support for team goals.
- *Recharge and reenergize* means you know the importance of rest and are not afraid to get the proper amount of sleep needed to be an effective leader in today's business world.

Normal Sleep

Sleep, an active, organized process, is the restorative and rejuvenating phase of daily life. It consists of sleep cycles of about ninety minutes each, during which we cycle through light sleep and deep sleep. On a typical night, we go through four to five such cycles, and with each cycle, our REM (Rapid Eye Movement) sleep gets longer, deeper, and more restorative.

The sleep state includes two major types of sleep: REM sleep and non-REM sleep. Non-REM sleep is divided into three different stages, with stage three referred to as "delta sleep." In adults, non-REM sleep accounts for approximately 80 percent of their sleeping time, while REM sleep occupies 20 percent of the normal sleep experience.

Sleep plays a vital role in memory consolidation, information processing, and retrieval. Adequate duration of regular sleep is necessary to maintain normal levels of cognitive skills such as memory, speech, complex thinking, and creative problem solving.

Our Circadian Rhythm

Chronobiologist Franz Halberg coined the term "circadian," using the Latin *circa* (around) and *diem* or *dies* (day). Its literal meaning is "approximately one day." A person's circadian rhythm is an internal biological clock located in the hypothalamus portion of the brain. It regulates a number of biological, psychological, and behavioral processes over an approximate period of twenty-four hours.

Most of our bodily systems are subject to circadian variations. Bodily systems most affected by circadian variations include the sleep-wake cycle, the system that regulates temperature, and the endocrine system. The circadian rhythm is responsible for afternoon sleepiness and subsequent propensity for serious error and significant decline in our executive function. This afternoon dip in alertness is deeper and more prolonged in the presence of sleep debt.

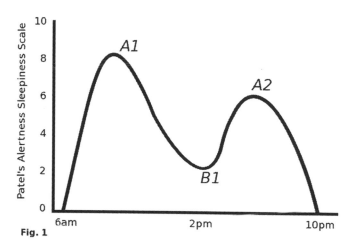

Fig. 1

The above graph represents a typical pattern of alertness seen in an executive who is an early-morning person. For an executive who is an evening person, A2 will be higher than A1, but B1 will remain the same. As a general rule, the toughest tasks should be handled at A1 and A2, and routine tasks at B1. As the sleep debt increases, A1, A2, and B1 will go down. The first goal of this book is to help you achieve rectangular alertness, defined as maximal alertness sixteen hours a day. This can be achieved through sleep hygiene discipline and Leader's Alertness Maximization Plan (LAMP), discussed subsequently.

You cannot improve what you cannot measure. And sleep deprivation impairs our ability to assess our alertness. The following is a quick way to assess how alert you are feeling at a given moment. Most of us are in the six-to-eight range of alertness, which unfortunately truncates our executive output and predisposes us to fatal errors. You should be aware of your alertness rating all day long so you can employ countermeasures to improve your alertness. You can also use your alertness rating to avoid task-ability mismatch and catastrophic errors in decision-making.

Patel's Alertness Sleepiness Scale Rating (PASS) (modified from Stanford Sleepiness Scale)

Feeling active, vital, alert, or wide awake	10
Functioning at high levels, but not at peak Able to concentrate	8
Awake, but relaxed Responsive, but not fully alert	6
Somewhat foggy Letdown	4
Foggy Losing interest in remaining awake Slowed down	2
Sleepy, woozy, or fighting sleep Prefer to lie down	0

REM Sleep Is Your Chief Innovation Officer!

REM sleep, the most active state of our existence, has a hyperactive brain in a paralyzed body. Chaotic and incessant neuronal firings characterize REM sleep, leading to tremendous physiologic activity and vivid dreams. Devoid of any constraints of time, place, or person, these vivid dreams spark innovation through out-of-the-world thinking. In the process, they help you create a world on your own terms. With a bit of practice, you can tap into this innovative power of your REM sleep.

Leaders Always Have a Vision

Leaders without a vision will never have followers. It's their vision that makes them indispensable to their followers and the human race. Abraham Lincoln dreamed of a nation free of slavery. Mahatma Gandhi had a dream of a free India. Dr. Martin Luther King Jr. dreamed of racial equality. Bill Gates dreamed of a computer in every house. Steve Jobs dreamed of a music player in everyone's hands. Amazon.com founder Jeff Bezos dreamed of the largest online bookstore in the world.

Your vision might be to create a breakthrough product, design a super-efficient supply chain, bring about disruptive innovation, or create a totally new market, or combination thereof. The problem is to find the right strategy and then execute it flawlessly. Can REM sleep help you do that? Can your night dreaming help you achieve the daytime dream that can change the course of human history? Yes, it can. The medical research has convincingly shown that dreaming during REM sleep can help you achieve your vision.

The Rat in the Maze

By using electrodes thinner than our hair, MIT researcher Dr. Matthew Wilson recorded neuronal firing in a rat's brain as the rat ran a maze. He continued this recording when the rat was asleep. To his surprise, he found the neuronal firing during REM sleep was identical to that when the rat was awake and actually running the maze. Interestingly, these neuronal bursts during REM were even more intense than they were during wakefulness.

What's more, while dreaming, we do not respect anatomical barriers. (In fact, the rat would run through the wall.) So, during REM sleep, you are not just thinking outside the box, but also running outside the box without the risk of banging into the wall.

Creativity after a REM Nap

Dr. Sara Mednik, a researcher at the University of California, San Diego, administered a Remote Association Test in which she gave participants three words and asked them to come up with a word that would link those three words; for example, given *sixteen*, *heart*, and *candy*, the answer would be *sweet*. After a nap containing REM sleep, participants produced a whopping

40 percent increase in correct answers, which strongly suggests that REM sleep enhanced the formation of associative networks and integration of unassociated information. This was after just a short nap containing REM sleep. Can you imagine the creativity after a full night of sleep containing a total of two hours of REM?

> "I think that these dreams involve a search for new and creative ways to put memories and ideas together," said Dr. Robert Stickgold of Harvard Medical School. "They can make associations that we wouldn't make when we're awake."

Studies have also demonstrated that our mood gets a real boost when we experience adequate amounts of REM sleep. Deprivation of REM sleep, on the other hand, can result in a depressed mood and affect.

The Historical Evidence Supporting REM Sleep

Otto Loewi, who received the Nobel Prize in 1938 for his work on the chemical transmission of nerve impulses, wrote:

The night before Easter Sunday of that year I awoke, turned on the light, and jotted down a few notes on a tiny slip of paper. Then I fell asleep again. It occurred to me at 6 AM that during the night I had written down something most important, but I was unable to decipher the scrawl. The next night, at 3 o'clock, the idea returned. It was the design of an experiment to determine whether or not the hypothesis of chemical transmission that I had uttered 17 years ago was correct. I got up immediately, went to the laboratory, and performed a single experiment on a frog's heart according to the nocturnal design.

There have been two Nobel prizes, inventions of numerous medications, and a plethora of very successful stories, novels, and pictures attributed to the crazy creativity of REM sleep.

Use REM and Innovate

How can you use REM sleep's crazy creativity to come up with disruptive innovation? Here are a few helpful tips:

- Accept the fact that we dream every night. We may not remember our dreams, but with training, we can learn to remember and even modify them.

- In the afternoon and in the evening, with positive emotions and unrestrained creativity, intensely contemplate on a major problem.[1]Ask for divine help by praying before retiring to bed. The Bible, in Matthew 18:23–26, says, "Have faith in God. I assure you: If anyone says to this mountain, 'Be lifted up and thrown into the sea,' and does not doubt in his heart, but believes that what he says will happen, it will be done for him." Praying helps us replace negative emotions, which are commonly associated with dreaming, with faith and optimism.

- Keep paper and pencil on your lamp stand. When you wake up at night to use the restroom, jot down what you were dreaming about and then go back to bed without thinking further. As soon as your eyes open in the morning, look at your dream notes and elaborate on them.

---

1 Harvard Medical School researcher Dr. Diedre Barrett has shown that, over 50 percent of the time, you can dream about what you choose to dream about prior to retiring to bed.

- Remember this key point, even if you do not remember your dreams: They do occur every night, and they consolidate your memory and rearrange your information database, helping you think more clearly and, in the process, find a more creative solution.

Invest in Sleep Hygiene and Maximize Your Return

Sleep doesn't differentiate us from animals, but sleep hygiene does.[2] And what is sleep hygiene?

Sleep hygiene is your personal set of habits that determines the quality of your sleep. Sleep hygiene helps you stay healthy by keeping your brain (most importantly, the executive center) and your body rested and strong. With poor sleep hygiene, you are not only getting insufficient sleep, but also poor quality sleep. In order to get the most return on your investment in sleep, you must follow sleep hygiene fanatically.

Unfortunately, poor sleep hygiene is commonplace in corporate America. Most of us stay up too late and get up too early. We often over-stimulate ourselves by working late into the evening and then watching television in bed. We may even use alcohol, thinking it will give us a better night's sleep. But alcohol, even though it puts us to sleep, causes frequent arousals and thereby robs us of deeper stages of sleep.

---

2 Michael Bonsignore regards sleep as a necessary evil or sunk cost, while Warren Buffet looks at sleep as the best investment one can make.

Like Any Investment, Sleep Hygiene Takes Discipline and Perseverance

The following tips will help you improve your internal rate of return from improved sleep hygiene:

- Create a sanctuary for sleep. Make sure your bedroom is dark. Even a little light can prevent you from falling asleep and getting enough deep sleep. This is especially important during long summer days and while traveling. Your bedroom should be a quiet place. Not only can noise prevent you from falling asleep, it can repeatedly awaken you at night and keep you from getting the restorative sleep you need. Ventilation and temperature are important. Cooler temperature is more conducive to sleep. Make sure your bedroom is cool and comfortable.

- Reserve your bedroom for sex and sleep only.[3] Do not take Excel spreadsheets and PowerPoint presentations to bed. Work in the living room or study, and when you are ready to retire to bed, go to your bedroom. While working, keep your laptop's brightness level down. Bright light can suppress endogenous melatonin secretion and delay sleep onset.

- Use the might of Mother Nature to your advantage. Going against Mother Nature by ignoring circadian rhythms will shorten your deep sleep (stage three and REM sleep). Always maintain a consistent time to rise, even when circumstances prevent you from going to bed at your normal time. And, yes, that includes weekends. There is no point in going to bed two hours late on weekends and waking up two hours late the next day. There is no net gain. In fact,

---

3 Several years ago, I was giving a talk to a group of nurses, and the slide read, "Use bed only for sleep." A naughty nurse reacted, "Where do we do the *other* thing?" Hence the modification!

there is a net loss, because it disrupts your intrinsic rhythm, the sole cause of reduced productivity on Monday mornings.

- Recognize that alcohol induces sleep, but a poor quality sleep marked by frequent arousals, leading to lighter sleep at the expense of REM sleep. In *Macbeth*, Shakespeare wrote, "It provoketh and unprovoketh." He was referring to the fact that alcohol provokes sexual desire but retards sexual performance. Similarly, alcohol induces sleep but robs you of your deep sleep. Because of this, the general recommendation in sleep-medicine practice is to avoid consuming alcohol six hours before bedtime. I try to be nice to my patients and request they avoid it within three hours of bedtime. You can start enjoying alcohol at five o'clock, stop drinking at seven o'clock, and go to bed at ten o'clock. A perfect evening!

- Make every effort to quit smoking completely, because it affects your sleep, too. Nicotine is a stimulant that would rob you of your deep sleep. But if you cannot quit, certainly avoid smoking within three hours of your bedtime.

- Avoid eating a heavy meal before bedtime; the process of digestion interferes with falling asleep and may reduce the amount of deep sleep. It also exacerbates acid reflux, which can further compound your sleep problems.

- Sweat for sound sleep. In ancient times, the harder one worked, the better one slept because it was physically demanding work all day. Your work, unfortunately, does not lead to better sleep because it is emotionally and intellectually, but not physically, demanding. This is where exercise comes into play. Regularly exercising, even for twenty minutes a day, has been shown to improve your sleep architecture. Not only does it make you fall asleep quicker, it also increases the duration of deep sleep and thus makes your sleep immensely more restorative. Exercising has such comprehensive health and performance benefits, especially for a leader, that it has become my personal favorite of all sleep-hygiene instructions. Please make every effort possible to incorporate exercise in your daily routine—it will make you a better corporate athlete!

- Stay away from caffeine, especially after one o'clock in the afternoon. Caffeine's duration of action is twenty-four hours, so a cup of coffee in the morning will still be lingering in your bloodstream when you are trying to go to sleep at ten o'clock. Some of my colleagues argue, "I can drink a cup of coffee and go right to bed and fall asleep." The fact remains, though, that it will still rob you of your REM sleep, making your sleep nonrestorative. Because of this, you will feel down and drowsy the next day, all day, and need more caffeine, which will again interfere with your sleep. This vicious cycle will continue through your career and lead to suboptimal leadership. Please taper off caffeine slowly over three to four weeks to avoid withdrawal symptoms. Switch to decaf coffee if you must drink it.

- Follow the two-twenty rule of napping. Do not nap after two o'clock, and do not nap for longer than twenty minutes. A ten – to fifteen-minute power nap in the early afternoon can energize your day and give you two days in one. But even a brief ten-minute nap in the evening will deconsolidate your sleep that night.

- Develop a relaxing bedtime routine. Listen to music. Read a nice book. Take a warm shower because the cooling-off process promotes sleep. Cookies and a glass of milk can help, too, because milk contains tryptophan, a naturally occurring sleep-promoting agent.

- Pray on the pillow. REM sleep is a powerful amplifier of emotions, especially negative ones such as fear, anxiety, hatred, and anger. To use this amplifier to your advantage, you need to focus on positive emotions all day and then, at bedtime, purge your mind of whatever negative emotions it has collected all day. This is where even a short prayer comes into the picture. Remember, faith drives away fear.

- Do not carry a grudge to bed with you. Bedtime is not the time to review your anger against others who have hurt you in some way. Luke 6:27–29 in the Bible says it best: "But I say to you who listen: Love your enemies, do good to those who hate you, bless those who curse you, pray for those who mistreat you. If anyone hits you on the cheek, offer the other also." Forgiveness always brings peace, and there is no better sleep aid than a soul at peace. Forgive yourself; forgive others.

Use Sleep Hygiene Score for Self-evaluation

How can you measure and then monitor your sleep hygiene? Here is a simple quiz designed for that purpose:

- Do you get at least eight hours of sleep every night, with a regular sleep/wake schedule, even on weekends?
- Do you use the bedroom only for sleep and sex?
- Do you avoid alcohol within three hours of bedtime and caffeine after one o'clock?
- Do you exercise at least twenty minutes a day?
- Do you pray before you go to bed?

Give yourself two points for each favorable answer. To earn maximum return on your investment in sleep, you have to score ten on the sleep hygiene quiz.

How Much Sleep Do We Need?

On *The Tonight Show*, Johnny Carson asked his guest, Dr. William Dement, one of the pioneers in the field of sleep medicine, "Why the hell do we need sleep?" Dr. Dement replied, "So that we don't feel sleepy the next day." Taking this logic further, we need to sleep so that we achieve and maintain maximal alertness all day long and capitalize on this alertness to maximize leadership and life itself.

Know Your Sleep Number

The need for sleep varies considerably among individuals. The average desirable sleep length is between seven hours and eight and half hours per day. For you, it could be seven hours. For your spouse, it could be eight and a half hours. As a general rule, whatever sleep length you need to feel maximally alert for sixteen hours all day the next day is the amount of sleep your brain needs to function at peak potential.

Avoid Imitation

My wife needs seven hours of sleep, but I need eight. Your chief financial officer (CFO) may need seven and a half hours of sleep, while you may need eight and a half to function at your peak potential.

Do not try to imitate when it comes to sleep duration. Your brain is unique, and you need to give it as much or as little sleep as it needs to perform at peak all day long.

"Yatin, I'm a Short-sleeper"

Based on a study done by Dr. Ying-Hui Fu and at his team at the University of California, San Francisco, the short-sleeper gene, a rare mutation, is present in only 3 percent of the population. And the majority of our leaders get less than six hours of sleep, certainly during stressful periods in their professional or personal lives. Dr. Ying-Hui Fu commented that while these people sleep less, we do not know if they need less sleep. We do not yet know if short-sleepers have increased long-term morbidity and mortality.

Researchers have also found that these short-sleepers fall asleep faster on a Multiple Sleep Latency Test (MSLT). In this test, subjects are asked to take five daytime naps, two hours apart. On average, a person who is not excessively sleepy will fall asleep in fifteen minutes. These short-sleepers fell asleep in less than ten minutes, a few even in less than five minutes, indicating their abnormal daytime sleepiness.[4] It has also been observed that these short sleepers take unplanned naps in or in between meetings, while traveling, and even at public gatherings.[5]

Less Sleep, More Life?

As a business leader, you may ask, "Can I invest less and make more?" It is a perfectly legitimate question. Van Dongen and others studied participants after four, six, and eight hours of sleep for fourteen days and found a significant dose-dependent decline in their neurocognitive performance. Belenky, Dinges, and other researchers have also reported similar findings.

---

4 Pepsi's CEO Indra Nooyi prides herself in sleeping only four hours every night. I would love to prove that she is excessively sleepy, by doing an MSLT in my sleep lab.

5 President Clinton was caught napping at the inauguration of the Clinton Public Library in his home state. On another occasion, at an event honoring Dr. Martin Luther King Jr. at Convent Avenue Baptist Church in Harlem, the former president was also caught nodding off.

In short, you certainly can achieve more by sleeping less, but at a significant health, cognitive, and behavioral cost. Thus, by sleeping less, you can read more, but you will remember less. You can check more e-mails, but your responses may not reflect your true leadership skills. You can interact with more people, but you might be less perceptive. You can work on more problems, but your solutions might be less creative. You can make more decisions, but they may not be correct ones. In short, if you are sleeping less, you might be a liability, as opposed to an asset.

"Sleep is for the weak, Mr. President," Secretary of Defense Robert McNamara said to President John F. Kennedy during the Cuban Missile Crisis.

My overworked colleagues, unaware of the research cited above, also continue to argue against sufficient sleep. Here is a list of arguments made by skeptics of sufficient sleep and my responses:

- *I don't need eight hours of sleep.* Studies have shown that restricting sleep to four or six hours (compared to eight hours) for fourteen days causes a dose-dependent decline in neurocognitive performance.
- *I only need five hours of sleep.* The short-sleeper gene, a rare mutation, is present in only 3 percent of the population (Ying-Hui Fu, University of California, San Francisco). The majority of leaders get less than six hours of sleep, certainly during a major opportunity or catastrophe.
- *I can fight sleep deprivation with strong motivation.* Motivation improves attention but not creativity, flexibility, mood, perception, and information management.
- *I have achieved a lot by sleeping less.* You could achieve even more by working on your alertness intelligence.
- *I don't perceive the deficit in my performance.* Sleep deprivation adversely affects prefrontal cortex (the executive center), which is essential for successful self-evaluation. This makes us unaware of our deficit.

- *I am highly productive.* You have increased your output as a worker/manager, at the expense of executive output.
- *The stakes are so high that sleep has to be on the back burner.* This is exactly the reason you should be giving sleep a top priority. Also, there are alertness-maximization techniques (discussed in sections II and III) that can help you.
- *I don't want to sleep away a third of my life.* Investment in sleep will enrich your life qualitatively, both at home and at work.
- *I will sleep when I am dead.* Unfortunately, studies have shown increased mortality associated with insufficient sleep. You must sleep eight hours every night if you want a successful career that can span five to six decades.

Procrastination: The Eternal Enemy of Sufficient Sleep

At some point or other, the common corporate ailment of procrastination has inflicted us. We have known the deadline for several weeks, but we find reasons not to work on that project until the last night, and then we pull an all-nighter and give an acceptable final product, but one that is far from being the best our creative mind can provide.

"I work best under pressure." We all have heard this, and it is true. But the problem is that when there is time pressure, we have adrenaline overflow, which increases our output but kills our creativity. We can analyze piles of data rapidly, discuss each point thoroughly, and put together the final presentation quickly, but the creativity is conspicuously absent. The big-picture vision is not there. The out-of-the-box thinking is still at home on our pillow.

Procrastination actually increases the energy required to complete a project. If project A requires x amount of intellectual energy, y amount of physical energy, and z amount of emotional energy, then, with procrastination, the same project will require the same amount of intellectual and physical energy, but a much larger amount of emotional energy because this incomplete, unpleasant task continually haunts your subconscious.

The energy required to complete **project A** $= x + y + z$. With procrastination, the energy required to complete **project A** $= x + y + z^t$, where t is time taken to finish the project. Why does this happen? It is the result of a psychological defense mechanism that compels us to avoid tasks that are unpleasant, difficult, emotionally demanding, or anxiety provoking. Maybe deep down we fear we will fail in providing a perfect presentation. Maybe we are afraid of failure and subsequent humiliation.

How Can We Conquer Procrastination?

Conquering procrastination is difficult, but here are a few suggestions to help you get started:

- Replace negative emotions with enthusiasm by using faith, peer support, and incessant activity, both physical and intellectual.
- Set pseudo-deadlines. I have found this immensely helpful when dealing with an unpleasant project. Tell yourself and your teammates that the deadline is a week before the actual deadline.
- Start small. A series of small steps will generate confidence and motivate you to finish the big project.
- Use "front loaders" first. If it is a team project, assign "front loaders" the task of researching and writing the preliminary draft, while

assigning polishing of the final product to the "back loaders." This way, at least the front loaders will present the project well rested.

A Fun Fact

Did you know that the second week of March is National Procrastination Week? Well, actually, it's the first week of March, but it is celebrated in the second week after a lot of procrastination. Happy front loading!

Good Time Management Will Give You Sufficient Sleep

If you want to lead with excellence, then you know you must master time management. How are your time-management skills these days? Are you one of those rare people who seems to have it all together and gets everything accomplished on your to-do list, and still have time left over at the end of the day? Following are some tips to help you find more time:

- Recognize that your time is exactly that—your time. If you are like most people, there are those in your life who have no respect for your time. Those include the people who are always asking you to do something for them. Until you learn how to just say no, they will continue to rob you of your time.

- Please yourself first, because you deserve it. Once you stop trying to please everyone else, you will start freeing up time in your own schedule.

- Look for ways you can combine tasks to save time. Simple things like reading the newspaper while riding the train to work, or taping your favorite television shows (and then fast-forwarding through the commercials) will give you more time. Be creative; see how many ways you can save time next week.

- If you are working on a project on a computer, resist the urge to keep checking your e-mail. Those e-mail distractions will keep you from getting your project completed on time.

- Turn off the television for at least an hour in the evening. Do not let the television networks control your nightly schedule. Be the true master of the remote control.

Discipline Will Result in Deep Sleep

Inadequate sleep hygiene is a major contributor to sleep disturbance and deprivation. Daytime sleepiness and difficulty falling asleep at night are solid indicators of poor sleep hygiene.

Sleep hygiene is just a matter of following simple and sensible guidelines. The result will help ensure more restful, restorative sleep, and promote greater daytime productivity and attentiveness.

Exercise Improves Deep Sleep and Executive Output

Busy executives complain they don't have time for exercise because their daily schedules simply will not allow it. After all, time is money, and most executives' time is committed from the moment they rise until they return to their beds. But exercise is a matter of choice, not time. Remember, we are all given the same amount of time: twenty-four hours a day, seven days a week. How you choose to spend your time can mean the difference between success and failure.

Sharon McDowell-Larson, an exercise psychologist for the Center for Creative Leadership, claims that executives who exercise are not only healthier than those who don't, but they also are more effective as leaders. She says, "Executives rate significantly higher on such skills as leading others (inspiring commitment, creating synergy, and interpersonally savvy), leading by personal example (specifically credibility), and results-orientation than non-exercisers." Being healthy and fit influences one's ability to lead. Not only does exercise promote health and fitness, it positively influences some of the most vital executive functions. Some believe that if exercise were a drug, it would be one of the most powerful medications on earth.

While it's true that busy executives would do well to consult their physicians before embarking on an exercise program, it is also true that those who park themselves while working from morning to night (at desks, in meetings, or in dens at home) should likewise consult their physicians.

The fact is that busy executives live their lives with an enormous amount of stress. How do they relieve it? Many don't. They believe that working harder to get the job done will alleviate their stressful lives. In reality, however, one job leads to another, and the level of stress never decreases.

Stages of Change in Adding Physical Activity to Your Life

Where are you? People normally go through a series of stages when it comes to physical activity in their lives. Those stages include thinking about it, preparing for some type of action, taking action, and keeping physical activity in their daily plan. The stages represent a spiral path to incorporating regular physical activity into your life.

Each stage takes time to acquaint yourself with new behaviors. All the stages need effort and commitment. You will move through each stage as you are ready to change. The interesting aspect of this model is that it recognizes you may not always move forward in a straight line. There will be times when you lapse, going back to an earlier stage; then the time will come when you are ready to advance forward. This is expected and part of the process of adopting new behaviors. You will progress when you are ready.

Too Stressed to Work Out?

Some use alcohol or prescription drugs to help manage their stressful lives. But even these are little more than futile Band-Aid attempts at solving the real problem, and if alcohol or prescription drugs are misused, they can create an even larger problem.

Many executives claim they are too stressed to work out. In fact, most are too stressed not to exercise. Focus and balance are needed when it comes to executive tasks such as goal setting, problem solving, communication, and team building. Exercise releases hormones that help you relax and bring focus back into your life. Exercise is a natural remedy that brings the body into a state of balance.

Following are some additional ways that exercise will de-stress your life:

- Exercise provides you with a mini-vacation that lets you escape from the stressors and pressures of the day. It gives you a period of solitude, when you can recharge your battery while contemplating important matters that need your attention. It can also be a time for creative thinking and problem solving.

- Exercise detoxifies. Psychosocial stressors cause a significant number of biochemical reactions in the human body. The fight-or-flight response brought about by stress causes the cardiovascular system to accelerate and the gastrointestinal system to slow down. In addition, certain neurotransmitters are activated, hormones are released, and nutrition is metabolized. Exercise detoxifies the body by eliminating the fight-or-flight response, thus allowing the body to return to homeostasis.

- Exercise releases endorphins, a naturally occurring morphine-like substance that provides pain control and euphoria. Negative emotions, such as fear and anger, whether expressed or repressed, play a major role in the progression of disease. Several notable research studies confirm this often-forgotten fact. Exercise offers a positive way to release the caustic energy of anger. It provides a healthy catharsis that allows you to dodge the otherwise devastating effects that anger can have on your physical well-being.

- Exercise boosts the immune system. The simple fact is, when fit people are injured or become ill, they recover faster because their immune system is stronger.

- Exercise improves deep sleep. Last, but certainly not least, exercise will help you fall asleep easier and sleep more soundly. Exercise improves sleep architecture and makes sleep more restorative. A short twenty-minute investment in exercise will improve your deep sleep so much that you will end up recouping that investment and more.
- Exercise leads to sustainable excellence. Exercise reduces your risk of an early death. Regular exercise improves your health by lowering the risk of developing high blood pressure, heart disease, diabetes, colon cancer, and depression. Regular exercise helps you control your weight while building healthy muscles, bones, and joints. It also reduces your risk of falling. A regular exercise program doesn't need to be a grueling experience, nor does it need to be time-consuming. You will experience excellent results through as little as twenty five minutes of strength training and thirty minutes of aerobic training twice per week. And the benefits will far outweigh the time invested.

Consider our ancestors. They did not have the health problems that accompany a sedentary lifestyle. To provide for themselves and their families, they had to work hard physically. As a result, they stayed strong and healthy. Today we lead sedentary lives that don't require much physical work, such as chopping, planting, tilling, harvesting, digging, and similar daily work activities. During our working hours, many of us sit at computers and monitor various aspects of our employer's business or our own. At home, we occupy ourselves with television, video games, the Internet, and other computer-based activities that do not require much movement. We need to get out of our seats and get moving. We need to rediscover the joy of an active and healthy lifestyle. If we do not, then disaster is waiting to happen.

Strong Muscles, Strong Leaders

Strength training helps us become physically stronger and achieve our optimum weight. To add resistance to the exercise, it uses equipment such as resistance bands, dumbbells, chin-up bars, and full-body weight systems.

As we age, we lose muscle mass. In fact, research has shown that after age thirty, we lose about 1 percent of our muscle mass each year. Strength training builds muscle mass that supports our skeletal system and keeps us mobile. Moreover, building muscle mass keeps our bones and joints strong, while slowing (and even reversing) the aging process.

Run and Lead

The American College of Sports Medicine defines aerobic exercise as "any activity that uses large muscle groups, can be maintained continuously, and is rhythmic in nature." An aerobic exercise overloads the heart and lungs, causing them to work harder than when at rest.

Many people think aerobic exercise only involves dance. While aerobic dance is a great way to exercise, other aerobic exercises are just as effective. These include swimming, stair climbing, running, jumping rope, fitness walking, in-line skating, cross-country skiing, and bicycling.

By using aerobic exercise to keep your heart rate elevated for a continuous period, you begin moving to a much healthier life. Aerobic exercise helps you use oxygen more efficiently by achieving and maintaining your target heart range, the safest range of heartbeats per minute during exercise. Calculate your target heart range by subtracting your age from 220 (for women) or 226 (for men), and then multiplying your answer by 60 percent and 80 percent. The lower number suggests a safe rate for beginners; the higher number is your goal as your fitness level improves.

Too Busy to Work Out?

If you're feeling too busy to work out, here are a few practical tips to help. You can find your own, too.

- Go from bed to bike in the morning. As soon as the alarm goes off, get on the stationary bike, and then check your e-mails and plan your day. Read your industry journal while pedaling the bike. You can buy laptop stands[6] that work well with bikes and even treadmills.

- Take the stairs during breaks. It will get your blood flowing, heart pumping, and mind going.

- Meet in the gym. Don't meet in the boardroom. Don't meet on the golf course. Instead, meet in the gym. Have a shoot-out on the basketball court. Use a punching bag to pound out your anger.

- Take a hike. Instead of meeting your production supervisor in the office, walk the floor of the factory. If you walk fast enough, you can get a good twenty-minute workout and also meet workers who would appreciate seeing your face.Play at noon. We used to have a racquetball league at the hospital where physicians would get together during their noon-to-one-o'clock break and play racquetball. This annihilates the midafternoon sleepiness, maximizes alertness, and improves executive output by at least 30 percent, in addition to destroying disastrous decision-making.

Please talk to your doctor before you begin any kind of physical exercise program. Share the kinds of exercise you're planning, as well as your outcome goals. Ask your doctor if your target heart rate calculation is appropriate for you and if there are any medical tests you need to complete before starting an exercise schedule.

---

6 http://airdesks.com has nice looking, functional, and affordable laptop stands.

Prayer, Positive Emotions, and REM Sleep

Busy executives from companies all across the United States believe in the power of prayer. Leaders who have a strong basis in their faith find it easier to meet challenges and overcome any obstacles that appear on their path. Plus, people who pray, especially before going to bed at night, tend to get a better night's sleep than people who don't. Prayer replaces toxic emotions with positive ones that are amplified during REM sleep, so you wake up in the morning with enthusiasm, energy, and optimism. If that's not enough to get you to your knees, what will it take?

Prayer Provides Personal Growth

"In the Company of Prayer" is an e-mail subscription service[7] created specifically for business executives. Through its "Morning Briefing" service, it delivers concise devotionals to the in-boxes of its subscribers each workday. Executive Editor Leslie Blanco says, "As workdays grow longer, time for personal growth, including in the area of spirituality, necessarily overlaps with the business agenda. A daily prayer prompt appeals to these executives who also appreciate simply being reminded they are in the company with others who share their emphasis on faith."

Morning Briefing subscribers really enjoy reading the daily e-mail devotions. Tim LeVecke, CEO of LeVecke Corporation, a bottler and marketer of distilled spirits, is one such subscriber. "The Morning Briefing is the first e-mail I open each day because it provides an opportunity for

---

7 You can subscribe for this service at http://www.companyofprayer.com/

a moment of personal focus and reflection that carries me throughout the day," LeVecke said.

The apostle Paul said we are to pray without ceasing. He also said we are to rejoice in the Lord always. That pretty much covers everything, but some biblical examples offer a little more insight. Daniel had the discipline of prayer firmly entrenched in his life, so much so that it cost him a trip to the lion's den. David started each day with his requests, anticipating God's answers so he could praise God at the close of the day. Jesus got up before the sun rose and went off by himself to pray. And the believers prayed when there was a need.

Pray on the Pillow and Pray on the Go

From a sleep and leadership standpoint, praying on the pillow (before sleep, after sleep, and at afternoon naps), along with on-the-go one-line prayers, works the best. Praying before sleep eliminates negative emotions. Praying after sleep prepares you for the day. Praying with your afternoon nap recharges your spiritual engine, while on-the-go prayers maintain your optimism during the challenges at work.

Prayer should be both a discipline that we exercise daily and a free flow of communication with God about whatever concerns us. Pray when you are stumped by a word or phrase, when you are up against a deadline, before signing a contract, and when turning in a manuscript. God's mercies are new every morning, so no matter how bad yesterday was, today is truly a new day in his kingdom.

Power Nap: Your Best Investment Ever

Winston Churchill said, "A nap in the afternoon gives you two days in one." While talking to Dan Rather of CBS News in 1993, Bill Clinton said, "If I can take a nap—even fifteen or twenty minutes—in the middle of the day, it is really invigorating to me. On the days when I'm a little short of sleep, I try to work it out so that I can sneak off and just lie down for fifteen minutes, a half hour, and it really makes all the difference in the world."

Because of our circadian rhythm, our alertness and, hence, our performance dips in the afternoon. This nadir is deeper when we are sleep deprived and when we are traveling across multiple time zones. If we can fight this drowsiness with a strategically placed power nap, then we can maximize executive function and avoid fatal mistakes. (Most fatal vehicular accidents occur in the midafternoon and after midnight.)

Studies prove that a fifteen-minute power nap provides benefits lasting up to 150 minutes, including:

- Improved alertness, both subjectively and objectively
- Reduced fatigue and improved vigor
- Enhanced creativity and problem solving
- Improved perception[8]
- Facilitated learning
- Improved declarative and procedural memory
- Positive mood and emotions, clearer communication, humor and optimism, and situational awareness

If a fifteen-minute nap gives you 150 minutes of improved executive function, how can you resist such an investment?

Power Nap: Wisdom, not Weakness

You have had a very busy week. You got barely five hours of sleep last night. Your day started at five in the morning. The schedule is tiring,

---

8 Using a functional MRI, a study by Dr. Sara Mednik showed that a nap prevents perception fatigue.

even for a seasoned corporate warrior like you. Opportunities are tremendous. Adrenaline is pumping. With meeting after meeting, phone call after phone call, and a hurried social lunch, it's two o'clock before you know it. And the board meets in an hour. You are expected to make a compelling case for a drastic change in the strategic direction that the company urgently needs. Your eyelids feel heavy. Neck muscles are tight. Information you have so painstakingly compiled does not look as clear as it did last night.

Can you present data clearly? Can you make your case passionately? Can you listen to their comments carefully? Can you gauge their mood? Can you perceive their interests accurately? Can you read between the lines? Can you separate people from the problem? Can you find common ground? Can you rally your colleagues for greater good? After a power nap, you certainly can!

But how do you take this power nap? Relax. It's easy. You don't have to do anything hard. Of course, there is a definite learning curve, but you will get better as you take these power naps on a regular basis.

In research studies, participants were asked to take naps in a quiet, dark, and comfortable environment. You may not have such an environment at work, but with practice, you can still take a very invigorating and rewarding nap. Legend has it that a ferocious Mughal warrior, Aurangzeb, took naps while still sitting on his horse in the middle of the battlefield.

The biggest obstacle to the practice of power napping is the stigma it carries in our frenzied corporate culture, which looks at napping as a sign of weakness, not wisdom. How do you take a power nap then? As with most changes, this one also begins in your mind. Review the reasons for power naps and the benefits they offer. Analyze the data and make a rational decision. Next, share your plan to invest in power naps with people around you, starting with your spouse, your secretary, your closest colleague, and so on.

As appropriate, educate your staff and colleagues about the performance benefits of power naps. Inform them that napping is a sign of wisdom, not weakness. This will help you overcome that cultural barrier and stigma associated with daytime napping. Then show the confidence of a leader and just do it. It is not that difficult; and it is worth the trouble and time.

Techniques of a Conventional Power Nap

The following tips will you help you rejuvenate your day with a fifteen-minute power nap:

- Proudly let your staff know that you will be taking a fifteen-minute nap. "Doctor's orders," you may add.
- Set your phone alarm, preferably on vibrate, to go off in fifteen minutes. An Australian study has shown that napping for less than ten minutes is suboptimal. More than twenty minutes can be counterproductive because of post-nap grogginess.
- Turn on relaxing music. You can try noise-canceling headphones. Bose are the best.
- Put on eyeshades. I find my Notre Dame cap very useful, especially when taking a nap in a public place; I just pull it down over my eyes, and I am off to the land of dreams.
- Stretch out on a couch or recline in a chair. Turn the chair away from people and toward the window or wall. A study from China showed greater benefit with stretching on the couch, as opposed to sitting.
- Close your eyes, shut off your mind, and relax.
- Wake up with a smile and vigor when the alarm goes off.

As we saw earlier, a nap containing REM sleep improves creative problem solving by a whopping 40 percent.

Remember that REM sleep has an active brain in a paralyzed body. Mother Nature made it so we do not act out our dreams. Also, studies have shown that REM sleep has a tremendous amount of random, bizarre, and seemingly unrelated activity, which our brain is trying to connect to make some sense of. Some researchers believe this is why a REM nap is able to boost creative problem solving; it links these random and totally unrelated activities together. This is the wildest and craziest form of thinking outside the box. Studies have shown that REM sleep plays a pivotal role in memory consolidation, too.

Can we do better than just lie down and relax for fifteen minutes? Can we modify our technique to make our nap more restorative, more recuperative, and more energizing? I think we can, by adding just a few steps to our conventional nap and making it a PREM (Patel's Relaxed Eye Muscles) nap.

Techniques for a PREM (Patel's Relaxed Eye Muscles) Nap

The following recommendations are based not on any specific scientific studies, but on my experience as a practicing sleep specialist and lifelong nap-taker:

- Before the nap, read a couple of lines from the Bible or another religious book. You can store them on your smartphone and read them before setting up the fifteen-minute alarm. Unfortunately, REM sleep, the sleep stage with vivid dreams, predominantly produces negative emotions such as fear, anxiety, guilt, and anger. This reading will help replace them with joy, optimism, love, and faith.
- Begin your nap with five to ten slow, deep, regular breaths. Control of breathing is control of life. Breathing, unlike heart rate, blood pressure, temperature, and gastrointestinal motility/secretions, is

the only vital function that we can easily control, and it is a time-tested tool used for centuries to achieve relaxation.

- Progressive muscle relaxation is incompatible with somatic anxiety. So, by focusing on respiration and relaxation, we are getting rid of anxiety, both from our conscious and our subconscious. As you breathe in and out, relax the muscles of your eyeballs and then continue to relax all the other muscles from head to toe and drift down into a state of pleasant relaxation. And when the alarm goes off, wake up with tremendous positive energy. I call this my PREM nap!

Conventional Nap	PREM Nap:
Slower cooling off	Rapid cooling off
Negative emotions	Positive emotions
Irregular respirations	Regular respirations
Incomplete muscle relaxation	Complete muscle relaxation
Untapped spiritual energy	Taps into spiritual energy

Open-eye Nap Is Not an Oxymoron

Once you have mastered the PREM nap, the next big challenge is to learn to take a PREM nap with open eyes[9] in a public place! Imagine you are listening to a long, dull PowerPoint presentation that is not going to help your cause, but you cannot get up and leave. Or you are done giving your speech, and as a courtesy to the other speakers, you remain until the entire function is over. You have a ton of things to do as soon as the presentation is done. Can you nap for three to four minutes at a time with your eyes

---

9 Vice President Joe Biden was caught napping during a budget speech by President Obama. He should have used the Open-eye Nap!

open, and use these minutes to recharge your executive engine? Why not? Fish sleep with their eyes open. A giraffe sleeps while standing. You can do that, too.

The Open-eye Nap does become easier after you have tried the PREM nap for a month or two, but for now, get started using the following techniques:

- Sit in a comfortable position. Sitting upright is fine. If the situation permits, you can slide down in the chair, too; just make sure the chair does not slide away.

- Pleasantly focus your eyes on the screen or toward the podium. Remember, when we sleep, our ears are open, and we still sleep well. Here, both your eyes and ears are open. With practice, you can successfully shut off your mind and relax completely.

- Take slow, deep breaths and relax from head to toe. Do not worry. You will not fall down. The tone of spinal muscles will hold you in the chair.

What if someone asks you a direct question? Do not worry. You will be able to wake up and respond, just as a sleeping mother can ignore everything else, but hears and responds to her child's crying in the next room. Before responding, you can say, "I'm sorry, I was still thinking about the excellent point you made earlier. Can you repeat your question please?" You can also ask a trusted neighbor or a team member to come to your rescue should there be a question or a comment directed at you. Just say, "Please tap my knee or shoulder if there is a question or comment I should respond to. I might be absorbed in some other thoughts."

Happy napping!

In this section, we learned about the importance of getting sound sleep of sufficient duration, and following sleep-hygiene instructions that can help us achieve quality sleep. In the next section, we will learn more about sleep deprivation and its deleterious effects on the leadership function. We will discuss common causes of sleep deprivation in today's corporate warriors and how we can treat them. So let's get started.

The High Cost of Sleep Debt

- ✓ Sleep Deprivation
- ✓ Epworth Sleepiness Scale; a Measure of Your Sleep Debt
- ✓ A Sad Case of Sleep Deprivation
- ✓ Sleep Deprived Politicians and Inventors

- ✓ Sleep Deprivation and Your Brain

- ✓ Insufficient Sleep Syndrome
- ✓ Inadequate Sleep Hygiene
- ✓ Obstructive Sleep Apnea
- ✓ Insomnia; Causes and Treatments

Sleep Deprivation

Sleep deprivation is defined as a sufficient lack of restorative sleep over a cumulative period so as to cause physical or psychiatric symptoms and affect routine performances of tasks. If your brain needs eight hours of sleep and it gets seven and a half, it suffers from quantitative sleep deprivation and resulting ill effects on leadership. Interestingly, if your brain needs eight hours of sleep and gets eight hours of poor quality sleep (less REM sleep percentage than normal) because of poor sleep hygiene, then it suffers from qualitative sleep deprivation. Most of our leaders suffer from both qualitative and quantitative sleep deprivation. They keep collecting sleep debt, which, unfortunately, is cumulative and cannot be paid off in one lump sum by sleeping in over the weekend.

How do you know how much sleep debt you are carrying? You can use the Epworth Sleepiness Scale (ESS) to determine the level of sleepiness you are experiencing because of cumulative sleep debt. ESS is a measure of chronic (long-term) sleepiness, while Patel's Alertness Sleepiness Scale (PASS) is a measure of sleepiness at a given moment. To find out your ESS, calculate your chance of dozing or sleeping in each situation described below. Use this scale to choose the most appropriate number for each situation:

0   would never doze or sleep
1   slight chance of dozing or sleeping
2   moderate chance of dozing or sleeping
3   high chance of dozing or sleeping

Situation	Chance of Dozing or Sleeping
Sitting and reading	
Watching TV	
Sitting inactive in a public place	
Being a passenger in a motor vehicle for an hour or more	
Lying down in the afternoon	
Sitting and talking to someone	
Sitting quietly after lunch (no alcohol)	
Stopped for a few minutes in traffic while driving	
Total:	

Add up the numbers to determine your ESS score, which is a measure of sleep debt. A score of ten or more indicates suboptimal function as a result of sleep debt. If you score ten or more on this test, you should consider whether you are obtaining adequate sleep, need to improve your sleep hygiene, and/or see a sleep specialist. You should discuss these issues with your personal physician.

Why is sleep debt important? Because it adversely affects every aspect of your life: professional, family, and personal lives. In fact, it affects your personal and family life even more than your professional life. When you are sleep deprived, you still have to do what you are paid to do, though it might be of suboptimal quality. There are enough support and layers of safety to ensure your work meets minimum safety and quality standards. But when you come home tired and sleep deprived, there is no such pressure to perform, no support system to help you, and no those minimum standards you must reach. So you may skip your son's basketball game, cancel your customary walk with your wife, or fail to enjoy quality time at the dinner table.

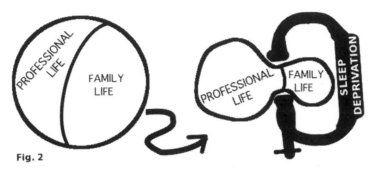

Fig. 2

Sleep deprivation shrinks a leader's professional life and to a much greater extent, family life.

A Sad Case of Sleep Deprivation

The first person to become internationally famous for self-imposed sleep deprivation was an American disc jockey named Peter Tripp, whose other claim to fame was inventing the Top 40. In 1959, Tripp managed the feat of staying awake under supervision for more than eight days and nights, for a total of 201 hours. He did it to raise money for charity, and did his broadcast live from a booth in Times Square in New York City.

As time passed, his friends and medical advisor found it ever harder to keep him awake. Constant vigilance was required to prevent him from lapsing into microsleeps. Three days into the event, Tripp became abusive and unpleasant. After the fifth day, he progressively lost his grip on reality and began to experience visual and auditory hallucinations. At one point, he even ran into the street, where an automobile nearly hit him. By the last evening, his brain-wave patterns were virtually indistinguishable from those of a sleeping person, even though he was apparently still awake.

After 201 hours of continuous wakefulness, Tripp had broken the record and halted the experiment. He immediately fell into a deep sleep that lasted twenty-four hours. When he finally did awake, his hallucinations were gone, and he felt relatively normal. But something seemed to have changed within him. Those close to him felt his personality had changed permanently and for the worse. His wife left him. He lost his job and became a drifter.

Getting enough sleep of the right quality and at the right time is essential for your health, happiness, success, and sanity. Sleep is the great leveler. Every day, it reduces even the most powerful and revered individuals—media celebrities, sports heroes, prime ministers, presidents, kings, queens, archbishops, and more—to the same inert and vulnerable state as the humblest and most underachieving specimens of humanity.

It Happened While They Were Asleep!

Following are some interesting characters and what happened while they slept:

- Delilah cut Samson's hair while he slept.
- Jack took advantage of the giant's slumber to steal his golden hen.
- Jason absconded with the Golden Fleece while the dragon guarding it was still asleep.
- The tiny inhabitants of Lilliput took Gulliver prisoner while he slumbered on the grass.
- Dracula sucked the blood of his victims as they slept.
- Odysseus and his men escaped from the cave of the Cyclops by putting the monster to sleep with strong wine and then sneakily plunging a sharpened tree trunk into his solitary eye.

Sleep-deprived Politicians

To get a glimpse of how sleep deprivation affects the human personality, think back to the last presidential campaign. Politicians from throughout the United States were on the trail, making speeches, kissing babies, and fending off negative ads designed to derail their campaigns. From early morning to late at night, these presidential candidates were giving it their all, with their lives under a microscope, and microphones, television cameras, and inquisitive reporters monitoring their every word. Yet, candidates admit the real difficulty on the campaign trail is not the pressure-cooker life that comes with running for president. It's the lack of sleep they must endure in the process.

"I won't remember Iowans," Mitt Romney commented in Altoona. His wife, Ann, corrected him. What Romney meant to say was, "I'll never forget Iowans." In Iowa City, Hillary Rodham Clinton said, "We had three hundred people outside literally freezing to death." Literally, no one had died.

Commenting on the killing of Prime Minister Benazir Bhutto, Mike Huckabee offered his apologies. No, the sleep-deprived politician didn't kill the prime minister, despite his apology. His campaign staff came to his rescue and assured the American people that the candidate meant to offer his sympathies. Huckabee later admitted that the pressures of the campaign had made it impossible for him to get more than four hours of sleep per night.

President Barack Obama said ten thousand lives were lost when tornadoes ripped through Kansas City. The actual death count was twelve. Obama blamed his overstatement on fatigue.

Sleep-deprived Inventors

American inventor Thomas Alva Edison was famed for, and frequently boasted about, his capacity to work very long hours with little or no sleep. Edison once made the astonishingly stupid remark, "There is really no reason why men should to go bed at all." On another occasion, he commented, "Sleep is an absurdity, a bad habit."

Perhaps if Edison had been smart enough to recognize the importance of sleep, it might not have taken him so long to invent the electric light bulb and the other gadgets he dreamed up.

Sleep Deprivation and Your Brain

Studies using both MRI and PET technology demonstrate that sleep deprivation diminishes activity in the prefrontal cortex. This area of the brain is responsible for several important functions, including empathy, mood, vision, communication skills, divergent thinking, and problem-solving skills.

Your prefrontal cortex is the real CEO. The prefrontal cortex, part of the frontal lobe, is the most active area of the brain in rested individuals. However, in sleep-deprived people, this part of the brain nearly shuts down. The majority of the deficits created because of these sleep-deficient shutdowns persist, despite strong individual motivation. The prefrontal cortex governs executive function, which includes our ability to:

- Make sound decisions.
- Predict the consequences of our actions.
- Remain goal-oriented.
- Conduct ourselves in a socially acceptable manner; that is, control our urges so as to avoid behavior that is unacceptable or even illegal.
- Plan, discriminate, make decisions, direct and sustain attention while ignoring distractions, and initiate goal-directed behavior.

- Have flexible and innovative thinking and decision making in response to novel and unexpected information and events.
- Integrate emotions and cognition to help resolve ethical dilemmas.
- In general, sleep loss results in:
- Lapsing, cognitive slowing,[1] memory impairment, and reduced vigilance[2]
- Change in mood and motivation, failure to complete routines, slower responses, physical exertion, and bickering
- Increased reaction time and decreased vigilance and attention
- Impaired working memory, verbal fluency,[3] logical reasoning, decision making, and judgment
- Decrements in innovative, flexible thinking, and strategic planning[4]
- Increased perseveration (trying failed solutions repeatedly) and lack of flexibility[5]
- Inability to focus on greater good, and resultant indecisiveness when faced with an ethical dilemma
- Inability to set ambitious goals
- Diminished problem-solving abilities
- Severely diminished ability to manage information
- Reactive instead of proactive response
- Diminished verbal fluency and communication skills
- Emotional agnosia (inability to recognize and manage emotions)
- Impaired mood, cognition, and psychomotor vigilance (makes you grumpy, foggy, and clumsy)

---

1 Slowed-down thought processes.

2 Vitally important for pilots, surgeons, and executives in a board meeting.

3 Our speech becomes incomprehensible at times.

4 Effect has been shown after one night without sleep.

5 Effect has been shown after one night of sleep loss, even on tests lasting less than ten minutes.

Because of the effect of sleep deprivation on the prefrontal cortex, sleep-deprived leaders lack the speed and creative resources to make quick, logical decisions and implement them well. These same studies indicate that a sleep-deprived person lacks the ability to consider multiple tasks simultaneously, which reduces the speed and efficiency of one's actions.

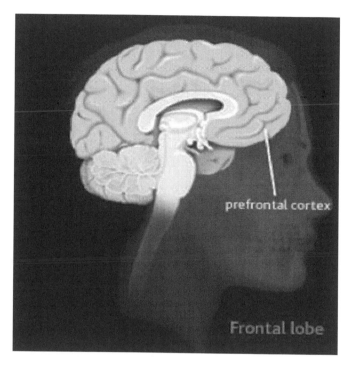

In studying the effects of sleep deprivation on the prefrontal cortex, researchers in the University of Iowa's Department of Neurology discovered that the prefrontal cortex of a sleep-deprived person functions much like a damaged prefrontal cortex. The only real difference is that sleep-deprived people have the ability to reset the prefrontal cortex's function simply by returning to a healthy amount of restorative sleep.

Every major study of the effects of sleep deprivation on the prefrontal cortex concludes that cognitive functions controlled by that area of the brain are severely impaired. Decision-making tasks, especially in an environment of uncertainty, are particularly vulnerable to sleep deprivation. A Harvard University study further suggests that age plays a major role in one's susceptibility to impaired functioning due to lack of sleep. The older one becomes, the more problematic this becomes.

The bottom line is that sleep deprivation significantly reduces brain activity within the prefrontal cortex. This reduction of brain activity makes it just about impossible to make a correct decision, especially when the outcomes are uncertain. Think about that the next time you make a major career decision or long-term strategic decisions about your corporation in the presence of sleep deprivation.

Common causes of sleep deprivation in today's corporate athletes are: insufficient sleep syndrome, inadequate sleep hygiene, obstructive sleep apnea, and insomnia. Let's look at them one by one.

Insufficient Sleep Syndrome

Insufficient sleep is the commonest cause of excessive sleepiness and resultant decline in leadership performance in the corporate world today. As discussed previously, both preventable and unpreventable sleep deprivation is highly prevalent, since leaders ignore both sleep duration and sleep hygiene. As they work longer hours year after year, they accumulate an enormous amount of sleep debt.

We have discussed the importance of sleep hygiene, procrastination and its prevention, and the importance of effective delegation and time-management skills to prevent insufficient sleep syndrome. Despite your best efforts, there will be times that insufficient sleep will be unavoidable. You can use tips provided later to maximize your alertness, emotional intelligence, informational intelligence, and, thereby, your leadership.

Obstructive Sleep Apnea

Obstructive sleep apnea, a serious and potentially fatal disorder, affects approximately 10 percent of the adult population. Snoring, daytime fatigue, witnessed apnea (cessation of respiration for more than ten seconds), morning headaches, dry throat, and waking up gasping for air are common features of this disorder, which is being increasingly recognized as a formidable enemy of corporate America.

Sleep apnea prevents a person from reaching deep, restorative stages of sleep, making the person grumpy, irritable, nervous, forgetful, inattentive, and tired. It also increases the risk of stroke, heart attack, and early death because of the nightly struggle to breathe, which causes frequent elevation of blood pressure and sustained drop in blood oxygen level, while simultaneously increasing the oxygen consumption of the heart muscles. Untreated, sleep apnea increases the risk of motor vehicular and industrial accidents.

Take the STOP questionnaire to determine your risk for obstructive sleep apnea:

S—Do you **snore** loudly?

T—Do you often feel **tired**, fatigued, or sleepy during daytime?

O—Has anyone **observed** you stop breathing during sleep?

P—Do you have or are you being treated for high blood **pressure**?

If you answer yes to two or more of these questions, then you are at high risk for obstructive sleep apnea and should talk to your doctor.

To get an accurate diagnosis, you will need an overnight sleep study in a sleep lab where your respirations, oxygen level, heart rate, EKG, leg movements, and sleep stages will be monitored all night long without using needles. The commonest and most successful treatment includes wearing a mask hooked to a machine, called continuous positive airway pressure (CPAP), which acts as a pneumatic splint and prevents your throat from collapsing at night. The other options are weight reduction, oral appliance (a customized denture that keeps your lower jaw pulled forward), and ENT surgery.

It is extremely rewarding to be treated for sleep apnea. Patients have told me:

- "Doc, I did not know how sleepy I was until I started wearing CPAP."
- "A hazy screen has been lifted off from my face."
- "I thought it was all stress and aging, but now I feel young again."
- "I am thinking clearer. I am planning better. I am getting more done at work and home."
- "I have so much energy that I don't know what to do with it."
- "My blood pressure is better; my sugars are better controlled."
- "I should have done this a long time ago."

If you suspect you have sleep apnea, please talk to your doctor. It will give you new life. If you need additional information, please visit my website (www.md4lungs.com) or watch my videos on http://www.youtube.com/yjpatel.

Inadequate Sleep Hygiene

Poor sleep hygiene robs you of your deep sleep, makes your sleep nonrestorative, and thereby reduces your return on the investment of your time. This is a case of an iatrogenic, or self-inflicted, injury, which, as explained previously, discipline, dedication, and persistence can prevent. Please follow those good sleep habits you learned in the section on sleep hygiene with discipline and passion.

At some point in their lives, more than a hundred million people complain about difficulty falling asleep, staying asleep, or both. The economic burden of insomnia is humongous, with estimates running to tens of billions of dollars every year. In *Macbeth*, Shakespeare wrote, "Uneasy lies the head that wears the crown." Why can't a leader sleep? What can a leader do? What about sleeping pills? When should you see a sleep doctor? We will try to answer those questions in the following pages.

Interpersonal Conflict Insomnia

One of the most common causes of insomnia in the workplace is interpersonal conflict. Interpersonal conflict is defined as an expressed struggle between at least two interdependent parties who perceive incompatible goals, scarce resources, and interference from the other party in achieving their goals. There are several causes of conflict. The most common ones are differences between people, needs, power, perceptions, principles and values, emotions and feelings, and internal problems and conflicts within a person.

Interpersonal conflict is everywhere today: conflicts between workers and supervisors, manufacturers and suppliers, two different departments, yourself and the CEO, and so forth. The cost of all this interpersonal conflict, while difficult to measure, is nevertheless incredibly high. Interpersonal conflict is at the heart of war, for example. It is at the heart of domestic violence, road rage, and hate crimes.

In the business world, interpersonal conflict has a tremendous negative impact on productivity, morale, employee turnover, and workplace violence. In schools, interpersonal conflict often erupts into violence and even death. Medical researchers have found direct links between interpersonal conflict and disease; psychologists have found similar links between interpersonal conflict and mental health.

Insomnia is a common symptom of interpersonal conflict. So what can we do? Given the fact that the world in which we live is literally filled with interpersonal conflict, it's obvious we can't always avoid it. How then do we manage it? When it comes to interpersonal conflict, here are some options you may want to consider: flight, fight, or unite. The choice is yours.

Flight means you can walk away. Interpersonal conflict can't occur if only one person is involved. It always takes two. To walk away is to ignore the conflict, even if someone is being physically threatening to you. Walking away sends a strong message that you simply want to avoid the conflict, at least for the present. The other individual may interpret your action in a variety of ways, however, and this may actually escalate the conflict.

Choosing to fight is rarely the wisest choice. Even the simplest interpersonal conflict will escalate if you choose to psychologically or physically back your opponent into a corner and act threatening. And violence always escalates into more violence.

The best way to deal with interpersonal conflict is by uniting with those who want to engage in conflict in order to solve differences cooperatively. Talking through differences using respectful language and unthreatening body language can resolve most any conflict.

While major conflicts may require professional third-party intervention, the parties involved can resolve most interpersonal conflicts. Make it a point to resolve them. You'll feel better, and you'll sleep better.

Workplace stress is one of the commonest causes of insomnia. The following are a few tips on managing stress successfully:

- Learn how to manage your time. Many people are stressed because they have trouble completing tasks on time. Look at your schedule and set your priorities.
- Learn how to deal with conflicts. When handling a difficult situation, keep your cool. When tensions are elevated, stress results.

- Learn to fit exercise into your daily routine. Exercise is a great way to relieve stress, so make sure you find time to get moving.
- Learn to eat healthy. Stop eating junk food for meals and snacks, and start eating healthy foods. Your body will cope with stress a lot easier. Reach for a piece of fruit instead of that bag of chips.
- Learn how to express your emotions. Talking to a friend or co-worker about your feelings is a great way to combat stress. Don't keep your feelings bottled up.
- Learn the importance of a good night's sleep. Make sure you find time in your busy schedule to make it happen.
- Learn to have a positive attitude.

Excitement Insomnia

Suppose that the innovative new product your team has been working on is ready for the big launch, which will open up new markets, increase your market share, put your company in the lead, and skyrocket your stock price. Prelaunch testing and research have all been positive. Popular media have given rave reviews, and they are covering the launch like the first iPhone launch. Your colleagues and your suppliers are all optimistic and excited about the new product. Can you turn off the adrenaline at bedtime? Can you shut off your mind when you put your head on the pillow? Can you sleep well during these times?

Here is another scenario: You have had a productive and very satisfying day at work. You are relaxing with your spouse. The kids are doing their homework. Then you get a text message from your star performer: "Sorry, I have decided to move on. I have accepted a job at another company." You knew this might happen, but did not expect it so soon and at a time when things were going so well for the company and for your star employee. You have been through this before. It does give you an opportunity to find someone with a different skill set, but in the short run, it increases your workload. "I can handle that, too. I'm not worried about this. I have built this company from scratch. I can tough it out until we can find someone good," you tell yourself. That night, you do not sleep well. The next morning, you wake up achy and tired.

Can you prevent this? Can you uncover anxiety when it is underneath the surface? And then can you successfully detach yourself from the troubles? Can you sleep well no matter what? You will have to, if you want to maximize your leadership during these exciting times. The following are a few helpful tips for those exciting or anxious times:

- Assign ten o'clock at night to six o'clock in the morning as sacred time, reserved for resting and recharging instead of planning and worrying.
- Get rid of all work-related material from your bedroom, including your laptop and smartphone.
- Continue your relaxing bedtime ritual: shower, relaxing reading, cookies and milk, and meditation, per your preference.
- Read your favorite lines from the Bible or any other religious book to calm your nerves.
- Turn off the lights and go to sleep.

Sweet dreams!

If you continue to have problems sleeping during exciting times, talk to your physician about using a mild sleep aid. This will prevent mounting sleep debt and, more importantly, prevent formation of an unhealthy conditioned reflex, which can perpetuate insomnia.

Treating Habitual Insomnia

Psychophysiological (learned) insomnia refers to continued difficulty falling asleep, even after the initial stressor has long gone. The whole experience of going to bed reminds us of the difficulties we had during those stressful days. We dread going to bed. We are anxious and therefore more awake when we try to go to bed. We keep on worrying about the impact this will have on our life the next day. Recognize it. Learn self-relaxation. Progressive muscle relaxation is an easy-to-learn and immensely useful technique. Reassure yourself that one or two bad nights are not going to paralyze your executive abilities.

Learn and follow these suggestions for sound sleep when suffering from insomnia:[6]

- Create a sanctuary for sleep. Bats sleep sixteen hours a day because they are in cool, dark caves. Make your bedroom dark and cool, too. Use darker colors on the wall. Hang relaxing pictures on the wall, ones of beautiful landscapes, gorgeous mountains, Buddha meditating, or the Baby Jesus sleeping in his mother's lap. Have dark blinds or heavy, dark drapes that block out light completely. Make sure the mattress is comfortable. If you like a firm mattress and your spouse prefers a soft one, then a Sleep Number mattress is the answer. Do the best you can to minimize noise. Soothing white noise can help promote deep sleep. Based on your preference, you can use the sounds of ocean, nature, or running water to achieve a similar effect. A recent study showed that keeping your head cool also promotes sleep.
- Learn a relaxing bedtime routine. A warm shower can help, because cooling off after a shower can be conducive to sleep. Listening to soothing music can calm your anxious nerves. A glass of skim milk and cookies can also help, because milk contains tryptophan, a naturally occurring sleep-promoting agent.

---

6 Relevant sleep hygiene tips are emphasized again here in this list.

- Go to bed only when sleepy, not just tired. Read a relaxing book. Listen to soothing and calming music.

- If you are not asleep after approximately twenty minutes, get out of bed. This will prevent formation of learned insomnia. Do something relaxing in the living room. Return to bed only when sleepy.

- Keep the clock face turned away. Looking at a clock at night will stimulate your brain.

- Don't fight Mother Nature. Even on weekends and even after a bad night, get up at the same time every morning. Use your inbuilt circadian rhythm to your advantage in this fight against insomnia.

- Avoid taking naps while going through insomnia treatment. If you must take a nap for emergency purposes, restrict it to twenty minutes or less before two o'clock for as long as possible.

- Use your bed only for sleep and sex. Ignore your laptop or smartphone completely when in the bed. When working on your laptop in the evening, keep the screen brightness to a minimum.[7] Watching TV in bed will stimulate your brain, too. Get rid of the TV in the bedroom.

- Recognize that exercise is the best ally of sound sleep. It helps us fall asleep quickly, stay asleep longer, and get more REM sleep. Even after a rough night, get twenty to thirty minutes of exercise anytime during the day, as long as it is not just before retiring to bed.

- Do not eat a big meal just before bedtime. The digestion process and acid reflux will both interfere with sleep.

- Avoid caffeine. Caffeine has a twenty-four-hour duration of action, so a cup of coffee consumed at seven in the morning is still in your

---

7 As mentioned earlier, bright light inhibits melatonin secretion from your internal pacemaker. This will make it difficult to fall asleep.

bloodstream at ten at night when you are trying to fall asleep. To avoid caffeine withdrawal, please taper off caffeine over several weeks.

- Absolutely avoid alcohol within six hours of bedtime while going through insomnia treatment. For patients not suffering from insomnia, the recommendation is to avoid alcohol within three hours of bedtime. Alcohol increases the number of micro-arousals (wakefulness activity of ten seconds or longer on an EEG recording) during sleep, robs you of your deep sleep, and makes your sleep nonrestorative. It also causes adrenaline overstimulation when the alcohol level in the blood is coming down.

- Do not take over-the-counter sleeping pills without consulting your doctor. An ideal sleeping pill is one that gives you six to eight hours of sleep with a normal percentage of deep sleep without causing daytime grogginess. It is also important that any sleeping pill you choose does not lose effectiveness with time and does not lead to dependence. Your physician can help you decide the right medication at the right dosage. Remember, you should not take a sleeping pill without knowing the cause of your insomnia. And when you do take a sleeping pill, take it at the lowest possible dosage for the shortest duration.

- If you are interested in herbal supplements, please read about valerian root, chamomile tea, and melatonin. You can visit the website of the National Center for Complementary and Alternative Medicine (NCCAM)[8] at http://nccam.nih.gov for more information. Chamomile is commonly used as a bedtime tea, but scientific evidence of its effectiveness for insomnia is lacking. The herb kava has been used for insomnia, but there is no evidence of its

---

8 NCCAM is the federal government's lead agency for scientific research on the diverse medical and health care systems, practices, and products that are not generally considered part of conventional medicine.

efficacy. The Food and Drug Administration (FDA) has issued a warning that kava supplements have been linked to a risk of severe liver damage. Valerian is one of the most popular herbal therapies for insomnia. Several studies suggest that valerian can improve the quality of sleep and slightly reduce the time it takes to fall asleep. However, not all the evidence is positive. One systematic review of the research concluded that, although valerian is commonly used as a sleep aid, the scientific evidence does not support its efficacy for insomnia. Researchers have concluded that valerian appears to be safe at recommended doses for short-term use. Some sleep-formula products combine valerian with other herbs, such as hops, lavender, lemon balm, and skullcap. Although many of these other herbs have sedative properties, there is no reliable evidence that they improve insomnia or that combination products are more effective than valerian alone. Remember that the FDA has not tested the efficacy and safety of these supplements. Discuss these with your doctor.

- Recognize that aromatherapy, using essential oils from herbs such as lavender or chamomile, is a popular sleep aid. Preliminary research suggests some sleep-inducing effects, but more studies are needed.

- Recognize that music therapy can help. Listening to relaxing music of your choice at bedtime can help, too. YouTube.com has a ten-minute music video by Dr. Jeffery Thompson with more than eight million hits and great reviews from people suffering from insomnia. (You can check it out by searching "Jeffery Thompson" on YouTube.com.)

- Learn progressive muscle relaxation. This is especially important if anxiety is contributing to your insomnia, because muscle relaxation is incompatible with anxiety. The technique is simple: Lie flat on your back in bed with your arms resting at your sides. Slowly breathe in and out. One by one, tighten and then completely and pleasantly relax each muscle, starting with the scalp muscle and moving down to the face muscles, neck, shoulder, chest, arms, abdomen, back, legs, and all the way to the toe muscles. You can repeat this process several times until you achieve complete relaxation. The goal is to achieve a sense of complete weightlessness through total physical and mental relaxation, and thereby eliminate anxiety. You can also try total relaxation, demonstrated in a ten-minute video on YouTube.com posted by Nancy Parker (coolkarmavideo is her YouTube.com user name).

- Learn mindfulness meditation. You can learn the technique on www.shambhalasun.com. You can also search for instructional videos on YouTube.com that teach to meditation techniques. A six-minute guided instructional video by Jim Malloy (jmalloy108) is extremely helpful.

- Consult your doctor if you have sleep apnea based on the STOP questionnaire, insomnia that persists beyond a week, have fallen asleep driving or come close to it, have fallen asleep during meetings, or felt sleepy and tired in the afternoon or evening.

Studies have shown that doctors, unfortunately, are the worst patients. They have an inbuilt reluctance to seek help when it comes to their own health. My colleagues in leadership positions are not much different. They are used to being in charge. They like to call the shots. They will tough it out. They will suffer. They will do everything but seek help from a doctor. "No one tells me what to do," they will say.

Please overcome that inhibition and see a doctor to design a plan of action; then stick to it. Your life, your family, and your stakeholders need you to be maximally alert all day long.

In this section, we learned how to measure our sleep debt using Epworth Sleepiness Scale. We also learned the deleterious effect of sleep debt on our executive function. Then we discussed common causes of sleep debt in corporate America today and what we can do about them. In the next section, we will learn to lead well during a major crisis or a tremendous opportunity, when sleep debt is unavoidable.

Leading Well Despite Sleep Debt

- ✓ Achieving Rectangular Alertness
- ✓ LAMP (Leader's Alertness Maximization Plan)
- ✓ Emotionally Intelligent Leadership
- ✓ Impaired Interpersonal Intelligence
- ✓ Sleep Deprivation and Informational Intelligence
- ✓ Leadership, Decision Making, and Sleep

You have carefully and painstakingly assembled a talented team to design a breakthrough product that will change the rules of the game. You have been working day and night with them. Lately, you have been sensing a lack of harmony. Creativity has disappeared, enthusiasm is waning, and the project is slowly stalling.

A lot is riding on this project. The deadline is fast approaching. You are frustrated. You have tried everything to get things back on track, but nothing has worked. Seeking advice, you call your mentor. You describe the situation and the solutions you have tried so far to remedy the problem. "What do I do next? Do I postpone the launch again? Do I outsource part of the project? Do I replace the whole team or just a couple of teammates? Do I augment the team by hiring a couple of outsiders?" After a thoughtful pause, your mentor says, "You do not need to change the team. You need to change yourself."

It hits you hard, right in the middle. You have never been self-centered, inconsiderate, moody, unpredictable, and pessimistic. Yet you have become just that, and you have unknowingly infected your team with these negative emotions and crippled this high-performing team. You have never been like this before. This is not who you are. You are a much better person and much better leader than this. The truth is, your mounting sleep debt has eroded both your emotional intelligence and informational intelligence and, thereby, your leadership qualities.

Can you get back on track? Can you regain your social skills? Can you restore and enhance your empathy? Can you understand others' perspective? Can you infuse optimism into the team? Can you seek the right information? Can you distill tons of information and apply it to the task at hand? Can you make critical decisions, or better yet, empower your teammates to do that? Can your team finish the project successfully and happily? Can you be the catalyst for the team?

You certainly can. And this section will help you achieve just that.

Achieving Rectangular Alertness

As sleep debt increases, so does sleepiness. How can you fight this drowsiness when you cannot pay off your sleep debt because of the enormous challenges at work? In this section, I will give you practical tips to help you maximize your alertness when you are sleep deprived.

You can't improve what you can't measure. Monitor your alertness using Patel's Alertness Sleepiness Scale (PASS). For consistent executive excellence, you need to be at a ten all daylong. Be aware of subnormal PASS at all times.

Patel's Alertness Sleepiness Scale (PASS)	
Feeling active, vital, alert, or wide awake	10
Functioning at high levels, but not at peak Able to concentrate	8
Awake, but relaxed Responsive but not fully alert	6
Somewhat foggy Let down	4
Foggy Losing interest in remaining awake Slowed down	2
Sleepy, woozy, fighting sleep Prefer to lie down	0

LAMP (Leader's Alertness Maximization Plan)

All day, and certainly during critical moments, measure and monitor your alertness using PASS. The surest and most natural cure for a low PASS is sleep, but what do you do when you cannot get sufficient sleep because of a hectic schedule and unavoidable demands? You can use the LAMP (Leader's Alertness Maximization Plan) to regain your alertness and thereby your leadership. Going against the might of Mother Nature, you can summon the help of these seven friends and design a LAMP applicable to your situation:

1. Physical exertion
2. PREM nap
3. Bright light
4. Caffeine
5. Smart snacking
6. Massage
7. Faith (my all-time favorite)

Also, beware of the formidable foe in alcohol when faced with insufficient sleep and long days.

Exertion Enhances Alertness

Earlier, we discussed the importance of regular exercise on REM sleep and, hence, on alertness and the executive function. Here we discuss the role of physical activity in improving alertness when sleep deprived.

Learn How to Deskercise

On average, executives spend seven and a half hours per day sitting: in meetings, at their desks, in an automobile, or in boardrooms. Our bodies do not like staying still for long periods. That much sitting causes tension to build. Muscles become tight, and joints become stiff. Alertness starts declining the longer you stay still. One way to prevent these otherwise inevitable results of physical inactivity is to "deskercise" every hour.

Deskercising will help you reduce muscle tension and stress, while also helping you preserve the flexibility, strength, and muscle tone you already have. The following are some simple deskercising techniques to try:

- **Wrist muscle stretch:** Most executives spend a good deal of time in front of computer screens. Computers have become essential tools in the management of business. However, with this increased use of computers, executives are becoming more susceptible to carpal tunnel syndrome, an ailment that used to be the exclusive domain of secretaries and other office workers who used typewriters and word processors most of the working day. Carpal tunnel is a painful wrist problem produced by repetitive motion. When working at the computer, stop occasionally and deskercise using the wrist muscle stretch: Slowly stretch your wrist muscles by using a full range of motion. Joints that have become sore and stiff because of repetitive-motion activity will respond to slow stretches. Don't risk pulling a muscle by attempting the stretch rapidly; get the full benefit by doing the stretch slowly. Not only will this give you a well-deserved break, it will go a long way toward preventing carpal tunnel syndrome.

- **Pectoral stretch:** This is an easy stretch you can do at your desk. Simply clasp your hands behind you head, and slowly move your shoulders and elbows back. Repeat this a few times. It is a great way to stretch your pectoral and chest muscles.

- **Wrist flexion:** Using your left palm, gently apply force to the right hand, causing the right wrist to stretch toward the underside of the right arm. Hold it there for five seconds and then release and repeat on the left hand. Repeat the exercise five times.

- **Wrist hyperextension:** Using the left palm, slowly apply force to bend the right hand backward. Hold it there for five seconds and then release and repeat to the left hand. Repeat the exercise five times.

- **Sitting bend:** In a sitting position, with your feet flat on the floor, your knees about ten inches apart, and hands at your sides, bend over as far comfortable with your hands reaching toward the floor. Hold the position for five seconds and then slowly pull yourself back into a sitting position while tightening your abdominal muscles. Repeat four times. This exercise stretches your lower back muscles and hamstrings.

- **Vertical stretches:** Vertical stretches provide an excellent way to reduce tension and activate all your major muscle groups. With your feet shoulder-width apart, lift yourself upward on your toes and extend your arms over your head. Reach each hand as high as possible for about seven seconds and then relax. Repeat four times.

Get Up and Walk Around

Sitting too long can have several negative effects. It puts stress on the lower back and can lead to muscle atrophy and diminished flexibility. It's important to get up and walk around at least once each hour. A ten-minute walk around the office would be excellent. But, when that's not possible, shorter walks to the water cooler, filing cabinet, or restroom are better than nothing. Even when you're involved in meetings, seminars, or workshops, get up at least once every twenty minutes and move around. You'll feel better, you'll be healthier, and you'll sleep better.

Other Elements of a LAMP

In addition to physical exertion, use other key elements of a LAMP to maximize your alertness. Following are some tips for doing so:

- **A PREM nap** can improve alertness for three hours. Studies have shown that a fifteen-minute nap can improve alertness and last for almost three hours. For specifics about PREM naps, refer to a discussion of it in Section I.

- **Massage**, especially when combined with a PREM nap, can improve alertness because it relieves muscle aches, back pain, headaches, burning in the eyes, and other distracting physical symptoms caused by sleep deprivation. Untreated, these symptoms can drag your energy level and your alertness down.

- **Caffeine** has alerting properties, but it continues acting for twenty-four hours, so a cup of coffee consumed at one o'clock in the afternoon is still in your bloodstream at midnight when your brain is trying to get into REM sleep. For this reason, caffeine should not be used indiscriminately, but rather as a medicine, at the right dosage, at the right time, and for the right reason. The surest indication for caffeine is driving when sleep deprived. Then it can be lifesaving.

- **Bright light** has tremendous alerting influence. Use this to your advantage. Sit facing the window. During long meetings in the boardroom, look up at light often. Especially on cloudy days, put a bright-light lamp behind your desktop while working on it. Every fifteen minutes, turn off the PowerPoint presentation and turn on the lights.

- **Small protein snacks** every two to three hours will maintain your energy and alertness; on the other hand, eating a large starchy meal will degrade your alertness. Grilled fish or chicken is fine. Avoid rice, pasta, and dessert.

- **Spiritual support** has helped me the most during my post-call days in the clinic. Going from one exam room to the next, I would look up and ask for divine help. "Give me energy, my Lord, to serve my patients well."

- **Avoid alcohol.** Even the legal limit of alcohol will impair your leadership when you are sleep deprived. When there is still work to be done, avoid even a small glass of wine or a beer. Resist that temptation.

Here is a summary of the recommendations just discussed for a Leader's Alertness Maximization Plan (LAMP):

- Keep moving.
- Face the light.
- Take a PREM nap.
- Get a relaxing massage.
- Snack smartly.
- Consume caffeine judiciously.
- Seek spiritual support.
- Avoid alcohol.

How to Become a Morning Person

The executives who are evening person find it difficult to get started in the morning. As a result, they end up missing out on 10 percent to 20 percent of the day and, in fact, of life, not to mention the potential for disastrous leadership while running early morning meetings. Here are a few tips that can help you become a morning person:

- As soon as your alarm goes off, get out of bed. Do not think. If you start thinking, you have lost the battle. Just get out of the bed.

- Go from the bed to bike and start pedaling. It can be immensely energizing. You can put your laptop on the stand and check your e mails and plan your day as you are pedaling.

- If you are a coffee person, enjoy a flavorful cup of coffee. You can set the coffee pot on a timer to start brewing fifteen minutes before your alarm goes off.

- A hot shower can awaken you, too. Make sure you get out of the shower quickly.

- Bright light in the morning can be extremely helpful. Phillips[1] makes an alarm clock that simulates sunrise. It works especially well on those dark winter mornings.

Eliminate Midafternoon Mistakes

Most mammalian species have a second sleep period during the daytime because of the midafternoon dip in alertness. This dip in the middle of the working day causes a decline in executive output and, more importantly, creates an environment conducive to disastrous mistakes. The following graph depicts the number of sleep-related accidents and their time of oc-currence. Please note the steep increase in accidents between one o'clock and three o'clock in the afternoon.

---

1 Philips Hf3470/60 Wake-up Light, Amazon.com (4.5 stars)

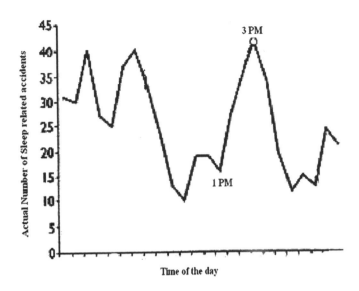

Incidence of sleep-related vehicle accidents (n=606) by hour of day BMJ 1995; 310: 565 Sleep-related vehicle accidents. J. A. Horne, professor, L. A. Reyner, research associate, Sleep Research Laboratory, Department of Human Sciences, Loughborough University, Leicestershire LE11 3TU.

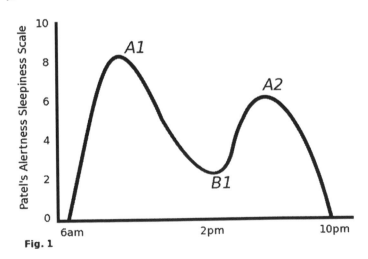

The above graph highlights circadian fluctuations in our alertness during a typical day at work. Remember that at B1, you are a liability, not an asset.

Intensive-care-unit rounds, board meetings, and important negotiations should be done at A1.

No matter what industry you work in, you will identify with the midafternoon madness that seems to take place among leaders and managers everywhere. Complacency and chaos tend to rear their ugly heads soon after lunch. Keep these tips in mind to help you get through the midafternoon madness:

- Take a fifteen-minute PREM nap in the early afternoon. It will go a long way toward improving your performance as a leader.

- Make sure you find a way to fit in thirty minutes of exercise each and every day, including weekends. When you do, you will drastically improve the quality of your sleep, which will ultimately make you a stronger and wiser leader.

- Eat a hearty breakfast, but a light lunch. If you avoid carbohydrates at lunch, you will not feel sluggish at the next afternoon meeting. Your brain will be able to think more clearly and handle crucial decision-making duties.

- If you receive an irate telephone call or e-mail, stop and count to ten. Avoid the temptation to fire back with anger and resentment. If you are sleep deprived, the situation will only become worse. Never let an e-mail or a telephone call get you so mad that you react like a child. Count to ten, take a walk around the block, or do whatever you need to do so you can respond with a clear and level head.

- When midafternoon madness strikes, do not make any long-term commitments.

- If at all possible, avoid scheduling any important meetings around the two o'clock time slot. Most people are so groggy from overeating or drinking at lunch that they will not be able to pay attention to important details.

- Keep moving. Get up and do some physical activity for at least ten to twenty minutes. It will help to keep the blood circulating and clear your head at the same time.
- Follow your Leader's Alertness Maximization Plan (LAMP).
- Avoid task–ability mismatch. Beware of doing high-complexity tasks or making important decisions in the afternoon.

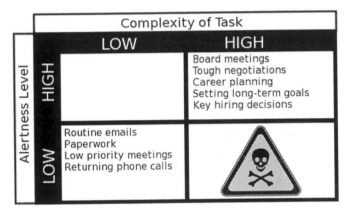

Fig. 6

Tackle routine tasks when you are low on the alertness scale and vital tasks when you are high on the alertness scale. Beware of tackling a high-complexity task when you are low on the alertness scale.

Regain Your Evenings

Early-morning leaders run out of energy and end up underperforming in the evening meetings. Here are some tips you can use to regain your evenings:

- Plan and take a ten- to fifteen-minute PREM nap prior to three o'clock. This will give you a second wind in the evening.
- Avoid heavy meals in the evening.
- An evening walk or exercise can be alerting. Get up and start walking as soon as you notice lethargy creeping in.

- It breaks my heart to tell you that even a glass of wine can drag your alertness down. Resist that temptation, especially if you have an important event in the evening.
- Caffeine can be alerting, but it will rob you of your deep sleep. It is best to avoid it.

If you follow above recommendations, you can achieve the rectangular alertness.

Rectangular Alertness

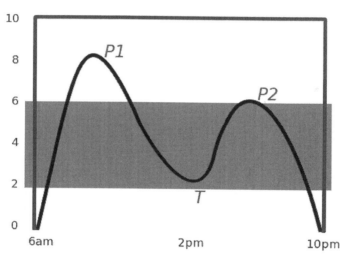

In the above graph, P1 and P2 refer to the peak alertness experienced by us in a typical day, while T refers to the trough in our alertness felt around mid-afternoon. By using the techniques discussed in this chapter, we can achieve the rectangular alertness and feel maximally alert all day long.

What are the benefits of the rectangular alertness? They are many, from the individual level to the national level:

- It can eliminate disastrous decisions and maximize executive output, both qualitatively and quantitatively.
- It can turn a good team into a high-performing team by eliminating suboptimal alertness and suboptimal performance during team meetings and beyond.
- It can ensure safety, quality, and optimum output by ensuring an alert workforce.
- Rectangular alertness can give the nation competitive advantage by having leaders and workers who are maximally alert all day long, even during a major catastrophe or a huge opportunity.

> Always lead from the highest level of wakefulness.

Emotionally Intelligent Leadership

So far in this section, we have discussed suboptimal alertness and countermeasures we can employ to improve alertness and thereby achieve rectangular alertness. Now we will discuss sleep deprivation's deleterious effects on emotional intelligence and countermeasures we can employ to overcome them.

The following list summarizes the deleterious effects on emotional intelligence:

- When sleep deprived, we are unable to accurately recognize emotions. Unfortunately, negative emotions are more readily recognized than positive ones.

- Studies have shown decreased subjective rating of happiness by sleep-deprived people.

- Our overactive fear center exaggerates our fear and anger when sleep deprived.

- Sleep deprivation impairs our social interaction and learning because of perception fatigue.

- A study from the Neuroscience Lab in Singapore showed that when sleep deprived, we are reactive and not proactive.

- Nervousness, irritability, and grumpiness hurt our teamwork.

- Impaired self-evaluation resulting from sleep deprivation makes us unaware of our deficits.

- Studies have also shown reduced motivation, increased risk taking, and indecisiveness when faced with an ethical dilemma.

Impaired Emotional Intelligence

Happy leaders have a higher net worth, but it is difficult, if not impossible, to maintain a pleasant demeanor and optimism when sleep deprived. Chronically running on insufficient sleep, we are grumpy, irritable, pessimistic, unpleasant, parochial, lethargic, complacent, and, hence, ineffective as a leader. This worsens when we encounter an unexpected challenge that unfortunately deepens our sleep deprivation.

Let's look more closely at the cause of impaired emotional intelligence and the countermeasures you can employ to overcome that impairment and be a happy, optimistic, enthusiastic, charismatic, productive, and influential leader. Remember, positive emotions lead to positive cash flow.

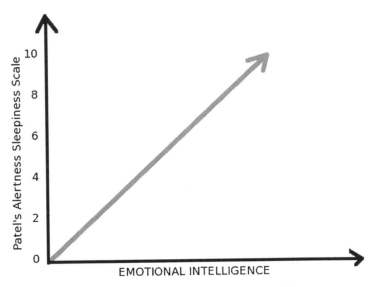

The above graph shows the linear relationship between our fluctuating alertness and our EI.

Fight-or-Flight versus Collaborate-and-Create

When you watch a scary movie, your amygdala, a primitive reptilian structure, is activated, but the prefrontal cortex informs it that this is not an actual threat. The prefrontal cortex calms down the amygdala in a split second, so we do not act on our fears. But when sleep deprived, if the amygdala perceives danger, it goes into overactive mode, unchecked by logical reasoning from a now-underactive prefrontal cortex, and it releases a large amount of adrenaline hormone, which sets the leader in fight-or-flight mode, as opposed to collaborate-and-create mode.

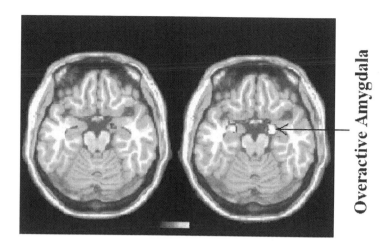

Overactive Amygdala

Brain scans showing amygdala responses to increasingly negative emotional stimuli in the control groups (left) and the sleep-deprivation group (right). (From *Current Biology* 17 (20). The human emotional brain without sleep: a prefrontal amygdala disconnect. Seung-Schik Yoo, Ninad Gujar, Peter Hu, Ferenc A. Jolesz, and Matthew P. Walker.)

For a moment, consider what this means, especially for those in leadership roles where others' economic, social, and physical well-being lies in the balance. A leader whose prefrontal cortex has been temporarily shut down could suddenly face an emergency situation where clear thinking and exceptional problem-solving skills are a must. What price would society pay for that particular leader's lack of sleep?

Irrational fears lead to severely suboptimal leadership. Monkeys are born with a paralyzing fear of snakes. But interestingly enough, when their amygdala is surgically destroyed, monkeys eat these snakes alive. Sleep deprivation makes the amygdala overactive, which further exaggerates our irrational fears.

How common are these fears among today's business leaders? During my Executive MBA program, at the beginning of our semester-long marketing elective, professor Phillip Raskin gave us five minutes to think about our biggest fear, write it on a piece of paper, and give it to him. He filed those papers in a folder and began his class. As the semester progressed, we got extremely busy with assignments and deadlines, and completely forgot about the informal study the professor had done of our fears. We were shocked and surprised when he shared the results in our last class. Forty-two out of forty-six students had written fear of failure as their biggest fear. Can you imagine the impact of this on our goal setting[2]? It can make a difference between Jeff Bezos staying in Manhattan as an investment banker or starting Amazon.com.

Imagine this fear getting further exaggerated from an overactive amygdala, the fear center. I remember going to our hospital strategy retreats after my seventy-two-hour ICU calls. Forget about suggesting and setting big, hairy, audacious goals; I was even afraid to set goals within our core competency. Be cognizant of truncated goal setting as a result of irrational fears.

Sleep deprivation also weakens one's ability to integrate emotion and cognition to guide moral judgments. A study showed that, when faced with an ethical dilemma, a sleep-deprived leader would have significant indecisiveness in making a decision in favor of the greater good, an effect that emotional intelligence partially neutralizes.

Impaired Interpersonal Intelligence

Have you ever considered yourself to be an artist? That might be a strange thing for a business leader to think about, but in reality, you are an artist who is in control of a business. And that business is made up of people. So it is very important that you, as an artist, can paint the right strokes on your canvas to come up with the finished picture you have been hoping for. As an artist, you have the ability to create a very successful business

---

2 This is the reason Facebook's corporate office has "What would you do today if you weren't afraid?" written on its walls.

environment that will allow everyone to work together toward a common goal: the success of the business.

The law of cause and effect tells us that, for every action, there is an equal and opposite reaction. We only get back what we put in. The same rule can be applied to managing people, and a good leader will recognize that fact of business life.

But as you undoubtedly already know, the art of managing people can be a chaotic and hectic science, no matter what industry you work in. In fact, I am willing to bet that 90 percent of the problems you encounter each week in your business are people problems. (I'm also willing to bet that the people who give you the most problems are not getting enough sleep.)

As a great leader, it is your job to determine what makes the people in your department tick, and do everything in your power to help them do their job the way they are supposed to. In the end, it takes a massive psychological effort to learn how to manage people with excellence.. Without people skills, you are dead in the water.

Mirror Neurons of Primitive Brain and Super Neurons of Leaders

Our brain is made up of a hundred billion neurons (nerve cells), each of which is connected to thousands of neurons through synaptic connections. Located in the frontal cortex, a small subset of neurons called motor command neurons fire when the person performs a specific action or observes someone else perform the same action. For example, when you try to open a bottle of wine or observe a friend trying to open a bottle of wine, the same set of neurons in your frontal cortex is activated. These are called mirror neurons.

Christian Keysers and his colleagues at the Social Brain Lab have shown that similar mirror neurons also exist for emotions. This discovery has great practical implications for leaders, because these neurons, once activated, can transmit both negative and positive emotions across the organization, making it a huge collection of neurons separated only by skin!

When exposed to our colleagues' negative emotions, our mirror neurons are activated in microseconds. What happens next has profound implications at the departmental level, corporate level, and national level. In the presence of sleep deprivation, an overactive amygdala, and an inactive executive center, a chain reaction starts, which recruits more and more neurons, leading to a viral epidemic of negative emotions.

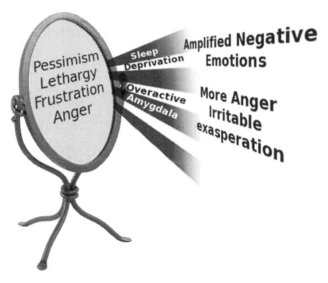

Colleagues' negative emotions activate our mirror neurons. An overactive amygdala amplifies these negative emotions, which rapidly spread across the organization.

Leaders Develop Super Neurons

How can you as a leader prevent such an epidemic of negative emotions? Even when faced with negative emotions expressed by followers, a well-rested leader with a well-regulated amygdala and hyper-vigilant executive center will recruit neurons with positive emotions. Here is the billion-dollar question, though: can we transform negative emotions in the presence of sleep deprivation, overactive fear center, and underactive executive center?

Yes, we can, by developing unconditional empathy toward everyone involved. The neurons responsible for such transformation are called super neurons. By nurturing and using these super neurons, a leader can rapidly spread a viral epidemic of optimism, innovation, ethics, integrity, exuberance, service, sacrifice, humility, euphoria, and success across a large organization—using mirror neurons. This is how Jeff Bezos sustained momentum and spread optimism at Amazon.com despite negative cash flow year after year. This is how Mahatma Gandhi spread his message of nonviolence, one neuron at a time, to three hundred fifty million illiterate Indians in the absence of a free press.

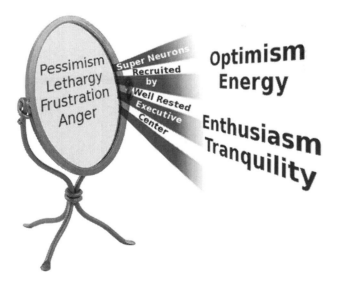

Followers' lethargy and pessimism reflexly activate a leader's mirror neurons, but a well-rested prefrontal cortex activates super neurons and transforms these negative emotions into positive ones. Because of these super neurons, leaders transform pessimism, lethargy, frustration, and anger into optimism, energy, enthusiasm, and tranquility.

Mirror Neurons and Mission Neurons

How often have we seen a stark disconnect between a company's mission statement as seen on its website and the actual values practiced in its corporate offices and manufacturing facilities? This disconnect is the result of leaders and upper management practicing a different set of values, which, by way of mirror neurons, are copied and disseminated throughout the organization. Therefore, avoid harboring and disseminating negative emotions. Instead cultivate and disseminate positive emotions across the organization, even when sleep deprived.

How do you measure and monitor your emotional intelligence? Here is a simple quiz:

Emotional Intelligence Quiz for Sleep-Deprived Leaders

If you answer five simple questions, you will know what your emotional intelligence score is.

1. Can you recognize your emotions?
2. Can you manage your emotions?
3. Can you recognize others' emotions?
4. Can you manage others' emotions?
5. Are your social skills at their best?

Give yourself two points for each yes answer and zero points for each no answer. The first two questions measure self-management. The next two measure interpersonal intelligence. The last one measures your social skills. Let's look at them one by one.

Can you recognize your emotions? When sleep deprived, we are sometimes too tired to care about recognizing and describing our emotions, but it can help us greatly if we can learn to accurately recognize our emotions. Look at the following list. Circle the words that represent how you are feeling. Accurately recognizing your emotions helps you manage them.

Embarrassed	Overwhelmed	Afraid	Excited	Angry	Annoyed	Fearful	Awful
Frustrated	Furious	Sad	Scared	Gloomy	Serious	Clumsy	Guilty
Shy	Confused	Stressed	Ignored	Stubborn	Impatient	Surprised	Tense
Jealous	Depressed	Lonely	Uncomfortable	Disappointed	Weary	Disgusted	Mad
Worried	Nervous						

Can you manage your emotions? Once you have recognized and described your emotions, the next step is to learn to transform the negatives ones into positive emotions. The following steps can help you do that:

- Diagnose emotions. Do not ignore them.
- Try to find the cause. You are impatient because you want to finish the meeting, go home, and relax. Or you are upset because your colleague has not done what he had promised to do. Or you are anxious because the deal you thought you had sealed might not go through.
- Seek support from your spouse. Remember, you have been through worse before.
- Have faith. Do a one-sentence prayer. Forgive yourself and forgive others. Learn mindful meditation.
- Sit straight and stand upright. An interesting study showed higher levels of testosterone and cortisol levels in participants who sat in a power posture than those who had slumped down in the chair.
- Walk with a bounce, and talk with a smile. A fake bounce and fake smile light up the same neurons as a genuine bounce and genuine smile.

Once you go through these steps, circle your emotions again. Hopefully, you will see some positive emotions now.

Embarrassed	Overwhelmed	Afraid	Excited	Angry	Fantastic	Pleasant	Annoyed
Fearful	Proud	Awful	Friendly	Relaxed	Bored	Frustrated	Relieved
Brave	Furious	Sad	Calm	Gentle	Safe	Caring	Generous
Scared	Cheerful	Gloomy	Serious	Clumsy	Guilty	Shy	Confused
Happy	Stressed	Comfortable	Ignored	Stubborn	Creative	Impatient	Surprised
Cruel	Interested	Tense	Curious	Jealous	Thoughtful	Delighted	Joyful
Thrilled	Depressed	Lonely	Uncomfortable	Disappointed	Loving	Weary	Disgusted
Mad	Worried	Elated	Nervous				

Can you recognize others' emotions? Sleep deprivation causes emotional agnosia, the inability to recognize others' emotions. To make matters worse, this selective agnosia makes us recognize negative emotions more readily than positive ones, resulting in pessimism and poor interpersonal communication when sleep deprived. How can we overcome this?

- Gather intelligence about their emotional intelligence. Know the emotional makeup of the attendees beforehand.

- Look them in the eyes. Remember, motor neurons fire when we watch others perform. Make it a habit, even when alert, to look into a person's eyes when talking and listening. Carry this habit forward, especially when sleep deprived.

- Listen more than you talk. Pause and perceive.

- Name those emotions. Use your newly acquired inventory of words. Find the right word from your memory to describe the emotions your colleague is going through.

Embarrassed	Overwhelmed	Afraid	Excited	Angry	Fantastic	Pleasant	Annoyed
Fearful	Proud	Awful	Friendly	Relaxed	Bored	Frustrated	Relieved
Brave	Furious	Sad	Calm	Gentle	Safe	Caring	Generous
Scared	Cheerful	Gloomy	Serious	Clumsy	Guilty	Shy	Confused
Happy	Stressed	Comfortable	Ignored	Stubborn	Creative	Impatient	Surprised
Cruel	Interested	Tense	Curious	Jealous	Thoughtful	Delighted	Joyful
Thrilled	Depressed	Lonely	Uncomfortable	Disappointed	Loving	Weary	Disgusted
Mad	Worried	Elated	Nervous				

Can you manage others' emotions? Use the following tips to help you deal with others' emotions:

- Acknowledge others' feelings. This can have a very calming effect on destructive emotions.
- Even in the face of insults, accusations, delays, and failures, maintain your tranquility. Only by maintaining evenness of mind can you manage others' emotions successfully and become a problem solver, as opposed to a problem creator.
- Find the root cause of the negative emotions, and explain your point politely and calmly.
- Offer a break from intense work. Offer to go for a cup of decaf coffee or to talk about something not so contentious.
- Practice, practice, and practice. Learn to manage emotions with enthusiasm and patience. Do it at every opportunity you get.

Are your social skills at their best? When we are sleepy, we are not at our best in social interactions. We are too sleepy to care, talk, or connect. How can you connect even when tired? The following are a few helpful tips:

- Smile and share happiness.
- Learn the big art of small talk.
- Express genuine interest in others' lives and interests.
- Relax and enjoy. If you *are* relaxed, you will appear relaxed.
- Look in their eyes when talking.
- Keep your arms open rather than crossed and closed. Positive body language is extremely important in your interactions with other people.
- Be humble and polite.
- Leverage your positive personality traits.
- Learn to pause and share your thoughts. Share your opinion clearly and politely. Be open to others' opinions.

- Identify what makes you uncomfortable, and then plan, practice, and enjoy.
- Record in your smartphone what their interests and hobbies are.
- Be patient. Improving your social skills is a slow process.

Even when tired, great leaders form lasting bonds.

Doctor's Orders

The following are steps to happy leadership when sleep deprived:

- Exude contagious enthusiasm and optimism. It will spread rapidly across the organization.
- Recognize that a smile is your savior. Humor and happiness stabilize a leader's intellect. Smile often. Stay close to people with positive demeanors.
- Recognize that pause is your partner. Pause before answering. Save emotional e-mails in the drafts folder and send them the next morning. If it is a complicated issue or a vital one, sleep on it.
- Do not dwell on the unpleasant aspect of your work.
- Pray often. When on the go, read a line from the Bible or other spiritual book.
- Replace fear and anger with faith and empathy through mental discipline.
- Avoid irritability. Take a walk, talk to your spouse, nap, meditate, exercise, and play. Beware of delicate situations that can exaggerate irritability. Tactfully avoid them or live through them quietly.
- Listen to the lazy one on your team or in your life.
- Look for collaboration and creativity.
- Set the goals high.

Thus far in this section, we have learned about rectangular alertness and emotional intelligence. Remember, happy leaders have bigger networks and higher net worth. Next, we will learn about information management in the presence of sleep deprivation.

Sleep Deprivation and Informational Intelligence

In *The Prince*, Nicolo Machiavelli wrote, "Because there are three classes of intellects: one which comprehends by itself; another which appreciates what others comprehend; and a third which neither comprehends by itself nor by the showing of others; the first is the most excellent, the second is good, the third is useless."

A leader can be the first kind, one whose intelligence comprehends by itself, by continually working on informational intelligence, which refers to the leader's insatiable thirst for relevant information and ability to retain, process, store, apply, and communicate this information in an easy-to-understand format. The leader will need a zen-like ability to quickly and continually distill a mountain full of information to find relevant information, given this era of information overload and information scarcity, when relevant information is buried deep under the mountain of irrelevant information.

Next, we will describe the deleterious effects of sleep deprivation on informational intelligence, and then give you countermeasures for overcoming the resultant deficit in leadership function.

As summarized in the following list, sleep deprivation adversely affects every facet of information management.

- When sleep deprived, we have a short attention span and suffer from easy distractibility.
- Studies have shown that our working memory,[3] procedural memory, and declarative memory[4] are also impaired.
- We are unable to consolidate and then retrieve memory when sleep deprived.
- We are also unable to incorporate new information into our decision-making.
- An interesting study gave participants sets of words like "hazy, cloudy, and dark." After sleep deprivation, they were asked if "black" was one of the words. Surprisingly, sleep-deprived individuals confidently gave wrong answers! Could this be the reason why honest people sometimes lie with confidence?
- Sleep deprivation also leads to rigid thinking and cognitive fixation (ignoring facts that do not agree with our diagnosis).
- Sleep deprivation causes a lack of verbal fluency.
- In a study using Master Planner Activity, sleep debt caused production misjudgment and loss of profitability.
- Sleep deprivation also impairs creative problem solving and causes perseverance error (trying an unsuccessful solution repeatedly).

---

3 It enables us to remember several pieces of information while we try to use it to solve a problem or carry out a task.

4 A memory that can be consciously discussed, or declared.

Impaired Decision Making and Loss of Situational Awareness

Air traffic control had cleared the airplane for takeoff on runway 22, which is 7,003 feet long and equipped with high-intensity runway lights; however, the crew mistakenly taxied onto runway 26, which is 3,500 feet long and unlighted, and attempted to take off. The airplane ran off the end of runway 26, impacted the airport perimeter fence and trees, and crashed. Of the forty-seven passengers and three crewmembers on board the airplane, forty-nine were killed, and one received serious injuries.

During its investigation of this accident, the safety board learned the air traffic controller who cleared the accident airplane for takeoff had worked a shift from six-thirty in the morning to twelve-thirty in the afternoon the day before the accident and then returned nine hours later to work the accident shift from eleven-thirty until the time of the accident at seven minutes after six the next morning. The controller stated that his only sleep in the twenty-four hours before the accident was a two-hour nap the previous afternoon between the two shifts.

Sleep Deprivation and Impaired Information Management

Bounded rationality, as described by March and Simon of Carnegie Melon University, refers to a leader's suboptimal decision-making as a result of paucity of available information, cognitive limitation of the brain, and time available to make the decision. In this era of information overload, paucity of information is seldom an issue, but cognitive limitation, especially cognitive slowing, is always an issue, and it unfortunately gets worse with sleep deprivation. Hence, the real challenge lies in our ability to rapidly filter and distill this information and then apply it for greater good.

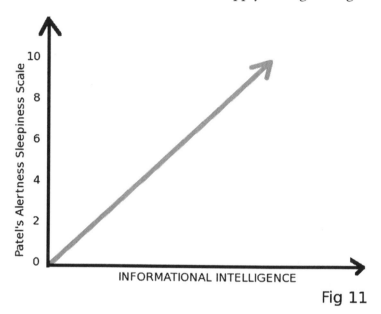

Fig 11

The above graph describes the relationship between alertness and informa-tion intelligence. As alertness fluctuates, so does a leader's ability to manage information.

In 2008, Duke University conducted an interesting study[5] to learn more about one's ability to manage information when sleep deprived. The study used MRI to measure blood flow in the brain during both normal responses and slow responses. The scientists found that, while a sleep-deprived brain can process simple visuals, "higher visual areas [those responsible for mak-ing sense of what we see] did not function well," according to Dr. Michael

---

5 The study was funded by grants from the DSO National Laboratories in Singapore, the National Institutes of Health, the National Institute of Drug Abuse, the NASA Commercialization Center, and the Air Force Office of Scientific Research.

Chee, lead author and professor at the Neurobehavioral Disorders Program at Duke. "Herein lies a peril of sleep deprivation." Chee further explained:

Study subjects were asked to identify letters flashing briefly in front of them. They saw either a large H or S, and each was made up of smaller Hs or Ss. Sometimes, the large letter matched the smaller letters; sometimes they didn't. Scientists asked the volunteers to identify either the smaller or the larger letters by pushing one of two buttons....During slow responses, sleep-deprived volunteers had dramatic decreases in their higher visual cortex activity. At the same time, as expected, their frontal and parietal control regions were less able to make their usual corrections. Scientists also could see brief failures in the control regions during the rare lapses that volunteers had after a normal night's sleep. However the failures in visual processing were specific only to lapses that occurred during sleep deprivation. The scientists theorize that this sputtering along of cognition during sleep deprivation shows the competing effects of trying to stay awake while the brain is shutting things down for sleep. The brain ordinarily becomes less responsive to sensory stimuli during sleep. This study has implications for a whole range of people who have to struggle through night work, from truckers to on-call doctors. The periods of apparently normal functioning could give a false sense of competency and security, when, in fact, the brain's inconsistency could have dire consequences. The study task appeared simple, but, as we showed in previous work, you can't effectively memorize or process what you see if your brain isn't capturing that information.

Sleep Debt Destroys Executive Excellence

Executive function of the brain includes complex cognitive capacities such as planning, organizing, initiating, sequencing, information processing, and working memory. Sleep deprivation has a major impact on the executive function, which is key to situational awareness, course-of-action determination, and discriminating between friend and foe. These are critical abilities for those in leadership positions. Sleep loss severely limits executive function, especially in the areas of creative thinking, sentence completion, estimation, and impulsivity. In a modern world that is only one misstep away from nuclear holocaust, a leader's ability to maintain executive function is critical. Adequate sleep is anything *but* a take-it-or-leave-it proposition. When we're tired and have important decisions to make, the best advice is to sleep on it.

Doctor's Orders

The following are steps to informed leadership when sleepy:

- Solicit novel ideas and suggestions. Methods should be flexible; goals may not be.

- Avoid internal distractions. Train your mind to stay focused on the task at hand. One pointed mind will achieve more at a majestic pace than a distracted mind at a frantic pace.

- Minimize external distractions. Discourage your colleagues from making distracting comments. Politely bring them back to the task at hand.

- Compile vital information in one location, as opposed to keeping it in various folders in various locations.

- Write, draw, write, draw, and remember. Verbal memory is more affected than visual memory.

- Prepare, write, and rehearse. Speak slowly and clearly. Avoid tongue twisters and long sentences.

- Scrutinize, verify, and dissect the data. At retrieval, sleep deprivation causes false memories.
- Seek simplicity. Bravely and mercilessly weed out unnecessary detail.
- Sleep on it if possible. REM sleep causes crazy creativity. Or listen to the lazy one on your team, or consult your spouse, parents, mentor, or well-rested buddy.
- Do not try failed solutions repeatedly.

Leadership, Decision Making, and Sleep

Are you a good decision maker even when sleepy? If you aren't or don't think you are, there is no need to worry. Decision-making is a skill that anyone can learn. Although some people may find this particular skill easier than others do, everyone applies a similar process. But remember the first rule of an effective leader capable of making the right decisions: get enough sleep!

There are two basic kinds of decisions: those that are arrived at using a specific process, and those that just happen, more or less in a blink. Although both kinds of decisions contain opportunities and learning experiences, there are definite advantages to using a specific process to make a decision. The most obvious advantage is the reduced level of stress you will experience.

Wise decisions are made using a definite process. They are based on the values and perceptions of the decision maker and include carefully considered alternatives and options, along with periodic reassessments of the decision and its effects. Wise decisions may or may not follow societal norms and expectations, but they are right for the decider based on what he or she knows at that point about his/her options, as well as about him/herself.

Eleven Steps to Wise Decision Making

The decision-making process outlined below can be applied to any situation where you need to make an important decision. If you follow these basic steps, especially when carrying sleep debt, you will find yourself making wiser decisions in your professional, as well as your personal, life.

1. Define, as specifically as possible, the decision that needs to be made. Is this really your decision, or someone else's? Do you really need to make a decision? If you do not have at least two options, there is no decision to be made. When does the decision need to be made? Why is this decision important to you? Who will this decision affect? What values does this decision involve for you?

2. Write down as many alternatives as you can think of. Brainstorm as many different alternatives as you can imagine. Let your imagination run free; try not to censor anything. This is not the time to be judgmental; just write everything down.

3. Think where you could find more information about possible alternatives. If you come up with only a few alternatives, you may want to get more information. Additional information generally leads to more alternatives. Places where you can look for the information you need include: friends, family, clergy, co-workers, state and federal agencies, professional organizations, online services, newspapers, magazines, books, and so on.

4. Check out your alternatives. Once you have a list of alternatives, use the same sources of information to find out more about the specifics of each option. You will find that the more information you gather, the more ideas will pop into your head. Be sure to write these down and check them out, too.

5. Sort through all your alternatives. Now that you have your list of alternatives, it is time to begin evaluating them to see which one works for you. Write down the values that would come into play for each alternative. Look for the alternatives that would allow you to use the greatest number of your values. Cross off the alternatives that do not fit into your personal value framework.

6. Visualize the outcomes of each alternative. For each remaining alternative on your list, picture what the outcome of that alternative would look like. It helps if you write out your impressions.

7. Do a reality check. Which of your remaining alternatives are most likely to happen? Cross off the alternatives that most likely will not happen in your situation.

8. Determine which alternative fits you. Review your remaining alternatives and decide which ones feel most comfortable to you. These are your wise decisions. If you are very happy about a decision but not as comfortable with its possible outcome, this is a clue that it is not a wise decision for you. On the other hand, you may dislike an alternative but be very excited about the possible outcome. This decision would probably not be wise for you either. If you feel you can live with both the alternative and the possible outcome, this is the wise decision you should follow.

9. Get started! Once you have made your decision, get moving on it. Worrying or second-guessing yourself will only cause grief. You have done your very best for the present. You always have the

option of changing your mind in the future. Remember, no decision is set in stone.

10. Review how it is going. Be sure to review your decision at specified points along the road. Are the outcomes what you expected? Are you happy with the outcomes?

11. Before making any decision, make sure you are not sleep deprived. Getting a good night's sleep is the most important thing an effective leader can do.

Use the countermeasures and tips discussed in this section on a regular basis to maximize your information management. Augment conventional education with continuing education to become the most knowledgeable person in the industry. IWith practice and perseverance, become the best speaker in the company so you can transmit that knowledge for the benefit of others.

In this section, we have discussed how you can be an effective leader even when sleep deprived. You can practice these interventions as it applies to your particular situation. For my post-call days in the clinic, I found the following Ten Commandments for the Sleep Deprived immensely helpful. I hope you do. In the next section, we will learn how to leverage maximal alertness to achieve consistent executive excellence and then how to maximize our God-given potential by incorporating the greed for greater good and spiritual fervor.

Ten Commandments for the Sleep Deprived

1. **Thou shall never make important decisions while sleep deprived.** If we all were completely honest, we would sometimes admit to making a decision when we were too sleepy to make sense of the situation. Never make an important decision when you are sleepy.

2. **Thou shall always speak slowly, softly, and clearly.** Verbal fluency is adversely affected when we are sleepy. We tend to eat our words, rush our sentences, and confuse our colleagues. Take it easy. Slow down. Speak clearly.

3. **Thou shall not get upset when the whole world does not yield to you.** Sleep-deprived people have this odd way of thinking. They truly believe that the sun rises and sets at their whim. They truly believe that employees will jump through hoops and bend over backwards, and they are quick to get angry when that does not happen. See what a lack of sleep can do to you?

4. **Thou shall stretch your body, gently massage your eyes, and take a timely PREM nap.** If you find yourself falling asleep at your desk, take action. Stand up, stretch your body, and gently massage your eyes for a few seconds. Then sit back down in your chair, and take a quick nap. You will be surprised what only a few minutes can do for your body.

5. **Thou shall strive for excellence in everything you do.** When sleep deprived, we have a natural tendency to just finish the work and head home without thinking about the quality of our work. So remember, in order to become an effective leader, you must strive for excellence and lead well even when you are sleep deprived.

6. **Thou shall be nice to yourself and reward yourself for excellent work.** When sleep deprived, we have a tendency to be critical of ourselves. Fight that tendency and congratulate yourself for excelling despite sleep deprivation. Reward yourself with a glass of wine or a relaxing massage at the end of the day.

7. **Thou shall postpone appropriate work for a well-rested you later on.** A great leader will not try to make decisions when too sleepy to think clearly. Presidents, heads of corporations, nonprofit executives, and others all have a history of saying, "Let me sleep on this." And guess what? It does work!

8. **Thou shall look for humor, smile often, and even laugh out loud, especially when things get worse.** If things are getting out of control and not working out the way you need them to, start looking at the brighter side. Smile, and try to enjoy the moment.

9. **Thou shall always walk away from a complex problem, an argument, or a tough adversary.** If you are too sleepy and find yourself in the middle of a complex problem that needs your immediate attention, find a way to walk away. There is no shame in saying that you need more time to make a crucial decision. A good leader knows the importance of walking away.

10. **Thou shall never eat a heavy meal when sleep deprived.** Have you ever been sleep deprived and then decided to eat a very heavy meal? Remember the outcome? It made your ability to make a sensible decision even worse, and, at the same time, it was damaging to your health. If you find yourself sleep deprived, instead of heading to the kitchen for a bite to eat, head to the nap room for some much-needed rest.

Just For Fun: Some Random Quotes about Sleep

- A good laugh and a long sleep are the best cures in the doctor's book. (Irish proverb)
- "Sleep that knits up the raveled sleeve of care; the death of each day's life, sore labour's bath. Balm of hurt minds, great nature's second course, chief nourisher in life's feast." (William Shakespeare, *Macbeth*)
- "Without enough sleep, we all become tall two-year-olds." (JoJo Jensen, *Dirt Farmer Wisdom*)
- "Finish each day before you begin the next, and interpose a solid wall of sleep between the two. This you cannot do without temperance." (Ralph Waldo Emerson)

Inspirational Quotes for Business and Work Excellence

- "The secret of joy in work is contained in one word, excellence. To know how to do something well is to enjoy it." (Pearl Buck)
- "The quality of a person's life is in direct proportion to their commitment to excellence, regardless of their chosen field of endeavor." (Vince Lombardi)
- "Excellence, then, is not an act but a habit." (Aristotle)
- "Desire is the key to motivation, but it's determination and commitment to an unrelenting pursuit of your goal—a commitment to excellence—that will enable you to attain the success you seek." (Mario Andretti)
- "The companies that survive longest are the ones that work out what they uniquely can give to the world, not just growth or money

but their excellence, their respect for others, or their ability to make people happy. Some call those things a soul." (Charles Handy)

- "Excellent firms don't believe in excellence—only in constant improvement and constant change." (Tom Peters)

- "The test of the artist does not lie in the will with which he goes to work, but in the excellence of the work he produces." (Thomas Aquinas)

- "Whatever your discipline, become a student of excellence in all things. Take every opportunity to observe people who manifest the qualities of mastery. These models of excellence will inspire you and guide you toward the fulfillment of your highest potential." (Michael Gelb and Tony Buzan)

AEImax Model of Consistent Excellence and AEI∞ Model of Supreme Leadership

- ✓ Medical Evidence for AEImax Model
- ✓ Ten Steps to AEImax Leadership
- ✓ AEI∞ Model of Supreme Leadership
- ✓ Seven Steps to AEI∞ Leadership
- ✓ AEIdash

AEImax Model of Consistent Excellence

Why is a leader great one day, average the next, and mediocre when crisis really hits? What makes executive output inconsistent despite the same ability, same expertise, and same brain? Is it just a statistical phenomenon based on the laws of probability? Does the performance have to assume a bell-shaped curve? Can you always blame macroeconomic factors for such inconsistent performance? How about factors within an individual? Could suboptimal alertness and resultant drop in emotional intelligence and informational intelligence cause this?

Inconsistent alertness leads to inconsistent leadership, and suboptimal alertness leads to suboptimal leadership. Studies have shown that maximal alertness can lead to consistent excellence. But since it is not always possible to be maximally alert, how do you maximize your God-given potential despite suboptimal alertness?

How do you recognize and overcome task–ability mismatch when a major crisis hits? When you are low on your alertness scale, hence low on your emotional intelligence score and your informational intelligence scale, how can you still be the best leader you can be? This is where the AEI program comes to the rescue.

> The goal of the AEI program is to maximize a leader's God-given potential and achieve true excellence, as opposed to truncated, suboptimal, inconsistent, and, hence, pseudo-excellence.

Medical Evidence for AEImax Model

As we learned earlier, our alertness fluctuates because of homeostatic drive[1] and our internal pacemaker, the suprachiasmatic nucleus, which makes us sleepy during midafternoon and at night. This decline is steeper and deeper in the presence of sleep deprivation.

The role of emotional intelligence in the leadership function has been well documented. What is overlooked, though, is the inconsistency in emotional intelligence, which contributes to the inconsistency in the executive function. A fluctuating level of alertness is the primary reason for emotional intelligence inconsistencies in the same leader at different times. Numerous studies have also shown that, as alertness declines, so does information intelligence (ability to understand, process, store, apply, and reproduce information).

We can reach an AEImax state of leadership when we maximize our Alertness, then leverage that alertness to maximize our Emotional intelligence and Information intelligence. Once we successfully eliminate internal factors responsible for inconsistency and truncated excellence, we can capitalize on external factors, both organizational and global. This is the state of AEImax, when the leader is at the peak of executive excellence, firing on all cylinders.

When you achieve the state of AEImax by design and discipline, you, as a leader, are in the zone. This is when you should make vital decisions affecting your own life or the company's long-term future, strategic planning, key personnel decisions, and mergers/acquisitions.

---

1 Alertness declines the longer one is awake.

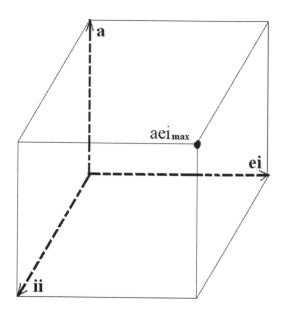

The above graph shows how one can, at a given moment, reach AEImax by maximizing alertness and then leveraging it to maximize EI and II.

Can you sustain this state of AEImax all day long? Can you be in the zone all the time? Remember, Mother Nature did not program our brain to be maximally alert sixteen hours a day every day. Also, today's global economy and executive expectations make it difficult to get eight hours of quality sleep every day of the year.

How can a leader be in the zone when the market crashes in Japan, volcanoes erupt in Iceland, or key financial institutions collapse? It is difficult, but not impossible, as we learned in detail in Section II. This long and rewarding journey toward being in the zone all the time starts with alertness intelligence, which begins with a fanatical discipline to follow sleep hygiene to maximize alertness. It also includes a continual and pleasant awareness of one's own and others' alertness, but most importantly, it involves learning and applying the countermeasures discussed in the Leader's Alertness Maximization Plan earlier. This will result in maximal alertness, which can last all day long.

Once you acquire rectangular alertness, you are ready to work on your emotional intelligence (self-awareness, self-management, motivation, interpersonal intelligence, social skills, and, most importantly, empathy). Developing unconditional empathy for your colleagues (especially those who do not agree with you), your customers (even those who complain about your product), your suppliers, and other stakeholders will help you become the best leader you can be. Follow the tips described in Section III to maintain empathy, optimism, enthusiasm, and social skills even when leading on insufficient sleep.

Next, you can work on your informational intelligence, which begins with an insatiable thirst for correct and useful information, along with the unique ability to receive, distill, digest, retain, apply, and reproduce it in an easy-to-understand manner. True leaders acquire almost a zen-like ability to focus on relevant information and zone out unnecessary information. They continually develop and use this informational intelligence to become the most knowledgeable person in the industry and the best speaker in their organization. Having achieved maximal alertness, emotional intelligence, and informational intelligence, you can proudly say that you are an AEImax leader.

> At all times, an AEImax leader is maximally alert, full of positive emotions, and the best informed and most knowledgeable person in the industry.

Ten Steps to AEImax

Reaching the AEImax state of leadership takes patience and perseverance. These recommendations will help you get started in the right direction:

1. Follow sleep hygiene with fervor. Guard your sleep like you guard your bottom line, because they are intricately tied together.

2. Develop alertness awareness. Throughout the day and at critical moments, use PASS (Patel's Alertness Sleepiness Scale) to rate your alertness.

3. With practice and persistence, eliminate preventable causes of sleep deprivation.

4. Expertly use countermeasures to neutralize midafternoon grogginess and jet-lag inefficiency.

5. Use PREM naps routinely to maximize your alertness and your leadership.

6. Continue to develop your emotional intelligence with a particular focus on empathy.[2]

7. Be pleasantly aware of your emotional intelligence throughout the day, definitely during the critical moments.

8. Learn to manage information effectively with special focus on distilling information for greater good.

9. Be the most educated and informed person in the industry by being a lifelong student. Remember that continuing education is infinitely more important than conventional education, as it is more relevant and more pertinent to the task at hand. By focusing on

---

2 I found Daniel Goleman's book, *Emotional Intelligence*, immensely useful. You can also attend seminars to improve your emotional intelligence. Or you can hire an executive coach who specializes in emotional intelligence training.

continuing education, dropouts such as Steve Jobs and Bill Gates excelled in their industry. Mahatma Gandhi rightly said, "Live as if you were to die tomorrow; learn as if you were to live forever."

10. Practice and improve your listening and public-speaking skills to be the best listener and speaker in the industry.

AEI-∞ Model of Supreme Leadership

You have trained your cerebral cortex for consistent and sustainable leadership through AEImax. Do you use this newly acquired asset for personal pride, profit, and prestige, or do you use it for greater good? If you use AEImax for greater good, as opposed to personal profit, can it elevate your leadership to unimaginable heights? Do you let your core competency restrict your goal setting, or do you use your faith and spiritual power to push your abilities to new heights? Would you let macroeconomic malaise keep you down, or will your deep faith push you to persevere? This is where selflessness and spiritual strength come into play.

Mahatma Gandhi was not the smartest lawyer of his time; Bill Gates was far from being the smartest student in his class. But what they had was a very narrow and well-defined passion that they used for greater good and an unshakeable faith that allowed them to maximize their contribution to the human race by persevering year after year, through ups and downs in their long but rewarding journeys. The following is a graphic representation of how an AEImax leader can achieve such remarkable feats using selflessness and spiritual energy to become an AEI∞ leader.

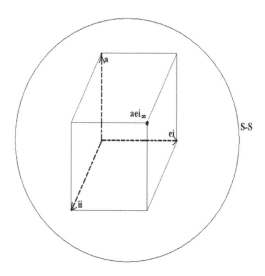

Selfless service and spiritual power will catapult your leadership from AEImax to AEI∞.

> There is no salvation but through selfless service. Selfless service and greed for greater good will transform your leadership.

Two young monks had to cross the river and reach the temple before sunrise so they could attend the prayer meeting that the visiting guru was presiding over. Excited about this golden opportunity for a rare spiritual experience, they took off in the early morning hours, arrived at the river, got in the boat, and started rowing toward the temple. When the sky became dimly lit before the actual sunrise, they discovered to their surprise and shock that the boat was still anchored and had moved only the length of the rope. This is, unfortunately, the typical journey for most of us. Unless and until we untie ourselves from this self-centered anchor, we will not achieve our God-given potential.

Anne Morriss of Concire Leadership Institute has studied leaders around the world and shared her findings in the *Harvard Business Review*. She found consistently in each case that, at some point in their career, these leaders had undergone a remarkable transformation, when they started thinking, speaking, and acting for greater good, as opposed to personal profit, pride, and prestige.

Long Journey to the Promised Land

Unsure of his direction, a motorist pulls over, shows an address to a teenager, and asks, "How far is this place?" The young man looks at the address and the direction the motorist is heading. "Twenty thousand miles!" After a pregnant pause, he adds, "But if you turn around, it is only two miles. The road is uphill and a little bumpy initially, but it is a beautiful and scenic route. I am sure you would love it."

Most of us are on this twenty-thousand-mile journey to our destination. We think constantly about our interests, goals, prestige, and profits. We need to change this from the root level up, and begin thinking about our customers, colleagues, company, country, environment, and human race. And when we do that, only then will we maximize our God-given potential and contribute to the advancement of the human race to the best of our ability.

Selfless Action: A Darwinian Paradox?

The most difficult internal struggle we encounter as leaders is the struggle between self-centered thinking and selfless thinking. Our natural inclination for the former stems from the survival instinct ingrained in our genetic makeup. Our overstimulated amygdala compels us to act on this reptilian instinct, which must be annihilated with the fierce power of the executive center, the prefrontal cortex.

Two main factors can help a leader fight this survival instinct: disciplined personal finances and a deep-rooted passion for the cause. Very few leaders can develop a passion reaching the depths acquired by Dr. King or Mahatma Gandhi; each man's passion made his survival instinct so obsolete that his fervor for his cause solely determined his actions. Developing a strong oneness with their cause can help leaders get started on this journey. Then persistence, passion, patience, and perseverance can help them become the selfless leaders they are capable of being.

You begin that journey internally, first by replacing self-centered thoughts one by one with externally directed thoughts. Have you noticed how industry leaders always think and talk about greater good? You can do that, too. Think of what is best for the department, company, industry, community, country, and human race. In doing so, you will grow as a global leader, you will be able to maximize your God-given potential, and you will reach AEI∞.

The 80/20 Rule of Selflessness

History is riddled with people who achieved greatness and served humanity, but ignored family responsibilities and ended up with a severely imbalanced life. Other leaders have maintained that delicate balance, and achieved the enormous feat of serving both their immediate families and the human race. You can successfully achieve this balance by following the 80/20 rule of selflessness. This rule recommends that you think, speak, and act for the greater good 80 percent of the time, and for yourself and your immediate family 20 percent of the time. This will help you achieve AEI∞ without the imbalance that can cripple your life.

How can you monitor and manage your selflessness? Use the following Selflessness Quiz to do so.

Selflessness Quiz

- Do you follow the 80/20 rule for selfless thinking?

- Do you follow the 80/20 rule for selfless speech?

- Do you follow the 80/20 rule for selfless action?

- Do you spend two hours a week doing charity work?

- Are you in contact with a selfless mentor?

Give yourself two points for each yes answer and zero points for each no answer. Ten out of ten is a perfect score.

Spiritual Strength: An Underutilized Asset

> If you say to this mountain, "Be lifted and thrown into the sea"
> and do not doubt, it shall be done for you.

"We Did Not Dream Big Enough"

The University of Notre Dame began on the bitterly cold afternoon of November 26, 1842, when a twenty-eight-year-old French priest, the Reverend Edward Sorin, and seven companions took possession of 524 snow-covered acres in the Indiana mission fields. In 1879, when a disastrous fire destroyed the main building, which housed virtually the entire university, Father Sorin vowed to rebuild the university and continue its growth.

"I came here as a young man and dreamed of building a great university in honor of Our Lady," he said. "But I built it too small, and she had to burn it to the ground to make the point. So, tomorrow, as soon as the bricks cool, we will rebuild it, bigger and better than ever."

That campus has grown from 524 acres in 1842 to 1,250 acres and 138 buildings in 2010. The University of Notre Dame today is a leading academic institution in the world. This would not have been possible without Father Sorin's unshakeable faith and deep spirituality.

Sleep deprivation adversely affects our faith and makes us ignore and, hence, underutilize our spiritual strength. We need to be cognizant of this handicap and find a routine such as prayer, regular meditation, frequent visits to our church, or continual consultation with our spiritual guru. Then we should stick to it, especially when setting our goals in life, planning our career, or facing adversity on our journey. Remember, faith sustains leadership.

This adverse effect on faith unfortunately gets worse with aging. Have you noticed how younger leaders demonstrate unbridled enthusiasm, set audacious goals, carry crazy creativity, and possess bold ideas? For most of us, aging, reality, and our work experiences moderate these qualities. Leaders, on the other hand, continue to nourish, nurture, and grow such enthusiasm and creativity throughout their long careers because of their deep faith. This unshakeable faith annihilates their amygdala's irrational fear and helps them reach their true potential.

The human race demands revolutionary ideas, actions, and results from its leaders. The only way a leader can deliver on this demand is by harnessing and utilizing spiritual strength. Deep faith and spiritual strength will help us see a future we can shape together for the advancement of the human race. Without faith and spiritual strength, Mahatma Gandhi could not have successfully sold his idea of nonviolence to three hundred million Indians, most of them illiterate, despite state-controlled media. When faced with insurmountable obstacles while working on our vision, a deep faith and spiritual strength will propel us past the problems.

How do you measure your spirituality? Here is a short quiz:

Spirituality Quiz

- Do you pray before starting your day?

- Do you pray before retiring to bed?

- Do you use a one-line prayer during your work?

- Do you go to a spiritual retreat every six months?

- Are you in contact with a spiritual guru?

Give yourself two points for each yes answer and zero points for each no answer. Ten is a perfect score.

Seven Steps to AEI∞ Leadership

How can we successfully get to the AEI∞ state of leadership? The following steps should help you get started on this long and rewarding journey:

- Disciplined personal finances will help your journey toward self-lessness. Make an effort to keep in touch with your friends and colleagues who practice simple living and high thinking. Frequently visit the website www.zenhabits.net, and moderate your urge to spend lavishly. Happiness does not come from owning, but from doing and giving. Self-indulgence that ties you up in a career you don't want is a noose around your neck. If you untie it and go for greater good, you will realize your God-given potential. Frugal families can serve a greater good.

- Solicit your spouse's and children's cooperation in your quest for greater good. They are your closest allies and strongest supporters. You will be amazed at how much cooperation you get when you patiently discuss your passion and demonstrate self-restraint, discipline, and willpower. This may not happen overnight, but with love, faith, and persistence, you will receive the cooperation and support of your loved ones.

- Look for common interests and actions that can help you personally and help your organization. Slowly advance this process as you follow the 80/20 rule of selflessness. Think, speak, and act 80 percent of the time for the greater good and 20 percent of the time for your immediate family. This rule will help you achieve supreme leadership without ignoring your family. Learn to think, speak, and act as a global leader destined to leave a legacy for generations to come.

- Humans learn best by observing. Mentor with a leader in the industry who has devoted his or her life selflessly to a noble cause. It might take patience, perseverance, and street smartness to find such a mentor, but you will be amazed by the number of true leaders who will find time in their busy schedules to teach their treasure of wisdom to a worthy devotee.

- Make a conscious effort to encourage selflessness in your colleagues. This will also help you in your own journey toward selflessness.[3]

- Choose a spiritual guru and keep in close contact. Attend a spiritual retreat every six months. Buddha said, "Be in the company of the wise, or better yet live with them."

- Develop a daily prayer routine. Pray in the morning and at bedtime. With immovable faith, read one paragraph from the Bible or any other religious book three times a day. When you are extremely busy and on the go all the time, you may not have enough time for a complete prayer, but a line or two on the go will suffice. "Come, Holy Spirit" is what Father Theodore Hesburgh recites religiously when he wakes up, before he retires to bed, and several times during the day. Such practice will recharge your spiritual engine and allow you to tap into that unending source of energy.

Serve, Pray, and Lead

At all times, an AEI∞ leader is maximally alert, full of positive emotions, and the best informed and most knowledgeable person in the industry. And this leader is continually striving for greater good with unshakeable faith and deep spirituality.

---

3 When he was engineering the company's turnaround in 2008, Howard Shultz, the founder and CEO of Starbuck's, took ten thousand store managers, against the advice of his management team, to New Orleans to volunteer. He later opined, "If we wouldn't have had New Orleans, we wouldn't have turned the company around."

AEIdash

How can you monitor and then improve your leadership skills? You have heard that you can't improve what you can't measure. My hospital CFO continually monitors total cash flow, asset turnover, net profit, and cash in the bank. The COO monitors patient census, length of stay, employee hours, and productivity. But no one monitors the most important and, unfortunately, most erratic of all—leadership ability.

Our amazingly simple, accurately reproducible, and extremely useful AEI∞ dashboard does just that. It provides instant, on-demand, visual feedback of your leadership capability at a given point in time. It also gives you an idea of where you are on your long and rewarding journey to AEI∞ and specifically what you still need to work on to get there. All you have to do is answer five questions each for alertness intelligence, emotional intelligence, informational intelligence, selflessness, and spirituality to get your AEI∞ score. It may appear complicated, but it is not. It will take less than three minutes the first time you do it, but after that, you should be able to do it on the go in between meetings without pencil and paper.

You can also download a smartphone application called "AEIdash." This app is very intuitive, simple yet accurate, and extremely useful. It measures your AEI∞ score with just a few clicks of the buttons and gives you real-time, colorful, and graphic feedback on your leadership ability in a dashboard format. You can store your AEI∞ score and graphically compare it with your prior scores. It also gives you an option of incorporating PASS (Patel's Alertness Sleepiness Scale), ESS (Epworth Sleepiness Scale), and Sleep Hygiene Score to make the process even more accurate.

Remember, you are your own CEO. Nobody will monitor your leadership skills and your career but you. Continually use AEIdash to achieve that.

To determine your AEI∞ score, answer the following series of questions:

Measuring Alertness Intelligence

- Have you been sleeping well for seven to eight hours for the past week?

- Did you sleep well for seven to eight hours last night?

- Are you feeling maximally alert right now?

- Can you sustain maximal alertness all day?

- Did you exercise for twenty minutes or more today?

Give yourself two points for each yes answer and zero points for each no answer. The first question checks whether you are carrying sleep debt; the second one, whether you are suffering from acute sleep deprivation. The third and fourth questions determine whether your alertness is maximal and sustainable. The last one measures your practice of sleep hygiene.

Measuring Emotional Intelligence

- Can you recognize your emotions?

- Can you manage your emotions?

- Can you recognize others' emotions?

- Can you manage others' emotions?

- Are your social skills at their best?

Give yourself two points for each yes answer and zero points for each no answer. The first two questions measure self-awareness and interpersonal awareness. The next one measures interpersonal intelligence, while the last two questions measure your social skills.

Measuring Informational Intelligence

- Can you receive information accurately?

- Can you process it effectively?

- Can you apply it appropriately?

- Are you the most informed person in the company?

- Are you the best speaker in the company?

Give yourself two points for each yes answer and zero points for each no answer. The first four questions measure your ability to acquire, process, and apply information to the task at hand. The last one measures your commitment to continuing education.

Measuring Your Selflessness Score

- Do you follow the 80/20 rule for selfless thinking?

- Do you follow the 80/20 rule for selfless speech?

- Do you follow the 80/20 rule for selfless action?

- Do you spend two hours a week doing charity work?

- Are you in contact with a selfless mentor?

Give yourself two points for each yes answer and zero points for each no answer.

Measuring Your Spirituality Score

- Do you pray before starting your day?

- Do you pray before retiring to bed?

- Do you use a one-line prayer during your work?

- Do you go to a spiritual retreat every six months?

- Are you in contact with a spiritual guru?

Give yourself two points for each yes answer and zero points for each no answer.

Now add up all your points, multiply the total by two, and you will have your AEI∞ score. One hundred is a perfect score, and when you achieve that you are an AEI∞ leader!

In this section, we learned how to achieve AEImax by leveraging rectangular **A**lertness to maximize **E**motional intelligence and **I**nformation management. We learned further how we start the noble journey from AEImax to AEI∞ by adding selflessness and spirituality. We also learned how to monitor our progress on this journey by using the AEI dashboard. In the next section, we will learn how these principles can be successfully used by negotiators, global leaders, female leaders, and our friends in radio and television journalism.

Advice for Special Situations

- ✓ Going to War When Tired: Can You Secure Peace?
- ✓ Leading from the Bag: Excelling Despite Jet Lag
- ✓ Female Leaders Are Unique
- ✓ Drowsy Driving Kills
- ✓ Watchdogs Can't Be Sleepy

The art of war is of vital importance to the State. It is a matter of life and death, a road to either safety or ruin. Hence it is a subject of inquiry, which can on no account be neglected.

Sun Tzu, *Art of War*

Going to War When Tired: Can You Secure Peace?

Picture this scenario: Your company, an eternal second in the industry in terms of market capitalization, has been frantically trying to acquire a smaller company, a significant player in the same industry, for almost a year. You are playing a pivotal role in this acquisition, which will put your company at the top of the industry in terms of market capitalization. It has been a taxing and exciting time for both the company (so it can finally get out of the shadow and be the leader) and you (propelling you to the top, where you belong).

You have been working day and night for several months, coordinating the efforts of various departments on both sides. You have carefully assembled a multitalented team of experienced overachievers destined to achieve this enormous feat. Adrenaline is pumping. Excitement is in the air. Emotions, both positive and negative, are high. You are continually acquiring and combing through enormous amounts of data. But in doing all this meticulously, you have accumulated a large sleep debt, which, unfortunately, is going to get worse as the weeklong negotiations start next Monday.

Can you manage and maximize your own and your team's alertness? Can you promptly recognize and manage negative emotions? Can you separate people from the problem as the negotiations continue? Can you look for collaboration and enlarge the pie? Can you look for greater good? Can you solicit, understand, and then incorporate new information? Can you analyze and present data clearly and correctly? When negotiations stall, can you paint a compelling and clear picture using concrete examples to galvanize the team and get negotiations back on track? Can you close the deal despite poor sleep? You certainly can. And this section will help you achieve just that.

Countermeasures for Suboptimal Alertness

Following are a few important points to help you maximize alertness when negotiating on insufficient sleep:[1]

- No one is going to fall asleep during these exciting times, yet everyone will be suboptimally alert because of preexisting sleep debt and insufficient sleep. Despite strong motivation to stay alert and attentive, microsleeps (ten to twenty seconds of sleep activity) can creep in unannounced during an important discussion.

- Pay up sleep debt the week before. Make a disciplined effort to extend sleep even by thirty minutes each night the week before. This technique, called sleep banking, has been shown to improve performance during the following week.

- Remember seven friends and a foe: use LAMP (Leader's Alertness Maximization Plan) as it applies to the current situation. During negotiations, move around. Take timely trips to the restroom or the snack cart in the room. Even while seated, keep blood flowing by doing ankle and knee exercises. Fight sleepiness with physical

---

1 These are the alertness maximization techniques applied appropriately to protracted negotiations.

activity, caffeine, and bright light. If conditions allow, take a PREM nap. You will be amazed how easy it is to find time for a PREM nap during even the most intense negotiations. You can sneak out for an invigorating nap when discussion is centered on a topic un-related to your area of interest and expertise. ("While you finance guys fight it out, may I take a fifteen-minute power nap? Update me when I get back, please.") This will do wonders for your alert-ness and executive performance for 150 minutes following the nap, without having any deleterious effect on your deep sleep—unlike caffeine—the following night.

- Schedule smartly. Avoid scheduling intellectually and emotionally demanding tasks for the midafternoon. They are better handled in the morning hours, when our circadian rhythm makes us univer-sally alert, even when carrying sleep debt. This is analogous to phy-sicians doing ICU rounds in the morning and leaving less critical tasks for the afternoon.

- Avoid starchy food. Small snacks every two hours will sustain your energy without putting you in a food coma. Avoid alcohol; even a glass of wine will impair your ability to think when you are work-ing on insufficient sleep. Reward yourself with a bottle of cham-pagne when negotiations are over. As Winston Churchill said, "In victory, you deserve it; in defeat, you need it." Manage your energy and the energy of all involved. Offer coffee breaks, walks, naps, bright lights, snacks, and encouragement.

Sun Tzu said, "If you know the enemy and know yourself, you need not fear the result of a hundred battles. If you know yourself but not the enemy, for every victory gained you will suffer a defeat. If you know neither the enemy nor yourself, you will succumb in every battle."

Countermeasures for Impaired Emotional Intelligence

What can you do to recognize and manage the emotions of everyone involved? This is the biggest challenge during intense negotiations between talented overachievers from different backgrounds looking at this complex process from their own interests and experience. The adrenal gland is pumping a large amount of adrenaline. To make matter worse, our fight-or-flight center, the amygdala (fear center), is overactive. And our executive center, which is supposed to counteract the fear center, is itself severely underactive because of sleep debt. The overactive amygdala's reptilian survival instinct will prevent everyone from seeing the bigger picture and will amplify the negative emotions, which, for the most part, are covert. These emotions rear their ugly head when sensitive issues come up for discussion.

Someone has to recognize and eliminate these negative emotions and, more importantly, amplify positive emotions and keep greater good on the table at all times. With proper planning and anticipation, you can predict some of these emotions and deal with them even before they arise. The real key to success is to maintain your own equanimity (evenness of mind) so you end up playing the role of a peacemaker, not deal breaker. Here are a few additional recommendations to help you achieve success when carrying sleep debt:

- Know their hot buttons. During prenegotiation intelligence gathering, pay particular attention to the emotional makeup and sensitive spots of the key players. This should cover the majority of emotional upheaval that can occur during the course of the event. Be pleasantly aware of your own sensitive spots and your own biases toward the sensitive issues and the attendees.

- Discuss sensitive topics in the morning, when alertness and, therefore, emotional intelligence are at their peak. Morning is also the best time to discuss topics of vital strategic importance or those of immense personal value. If, however, for scheduling reasons or otherwise, such a topic ends up on the table in the afternoon, there are ways you can be ready for it: Don't forget the seven friends and a foe. Sit facing the light. Stare at bright light periodically. Avoid a heavy lunch and alcohol. Take a PREM nap prior to the discussion. Move around. A trip to the restroom is fine, too. Stretch your legs often. A cup of coffee is allowed, considering the gravity of the situation. Refer to your notes regularly. Maintain eye contact while listening. Ask questions. Write before you speak. Smile, pause, and speak slowly. Keep discussion on a greater good (customers) without being too saintly, patronizing, or condescending.

- A study from Singapore showed that sleep deprivation makes us reactive, instead of proactive. Fight this tendency with a friendly smile and a pleasant pause before responding to an allegation or insinuation. Another technique that can help the process is asking questions. "Can you elaborate on that, please?" or "May I have some clarification on that, please?" Better yet, "Let us get some objective data on that." Then there's my all-time favorite, "Let me sleep on it."

- Recognize and promptly deal with waning optimism during protracted negotiations. Keep smiling. Nervousness, irritability, and grumpiness will creep in when you are low on the alertness scale. Be on guard against this. People like to work with people who are fun to work with. Joy and humor clarifies communication and creates a bond. Work on it, and keep on smiling.

- Sleep deprivation, unfortunately, makes it difficult for you to understand others' emotions and interests. Maintain pleasant eye

contact, especially with the key decision makers. Also make a conscious effort to understand others' interests.

> Now the general who wins a battle makes many calculations in his temple ere the battle is fought. The general who loses a battle makes but few calculations beforehand.
>
> Sun Tzu, Art of War

Countermeasures for Impaired Informational Intelligence

Paucity of information is never an issue in this day and age, but successfully combing through the mountain of data to find relevant and accurate
information is difficult for a sleep-deprived executive who, unfortunately,
is unaware of this deficit because of an underactive prefrontal cortex (executive center). Getting preoccupied with inaccurate or irrelevant information
or overlooking a critical error can also occur. You will be amazed by how
many diligent minds have overlooked critical information[2] or misplaced a
decimal point with catastrophic consequences.

Here are a few tips to help you eliminate informational-intelligence
impairment during protracted negotiations:

---

2 Here is a simple story that highlights the importance of getting the right information
while negotiating: A boy and his elder sister both want the orange, and in a distributive
approach, settle for half the orange each. However, if they talk to each other, they figure
out that the boy wants to eat the whole orange and has no need for the orange skin,
while the elder sister wants the orange skin as one of the ingredients for a cake she is
baking. Once they figure out what each wants, the boy gets to eat the whole orange while
the elder sister gets to use the skin from the orange. In the latter case, both get what they
really want without taking away anything from each other. This is integrative bargaining.

- Think fast. Stay flexible. Cognitive slowing and cognitive fixation (ignoring information that does not agree with your opinion) are common, too. You may have seen this firsthand when a colleague, who made a decision prior to reviewing all available information, remained immovable, regardless of how much data you subsequently presented. Make sure you solicit new information and stay flexible to incorporate it for greater good.

- Designate a creative problem-solver. Negotiations are breezing by. Your talented team is overcoming one hurdle after another. The team sees the light at the end of the tunnel. All of a sudden, an unexpected problem stalls the process. No one is complaining, but everyone is tired and sleep deprived. Everyone's creative problem-solving ability is down by at least 40 percent because of insufficient REM sleep. This is the perfect time to consult "a well-rested creative problem-solver." Most of the time, this is your mentor. It could also be your spouse, parent, or a well-rested colleague in your organization.

- Write, or better yet, draw your BATNA (Best Alternative To a Negotiated Agreement) on a piece of paper. Sleep deprivation, as discussed earlier, impairs our working memory, verbal memory more than visual memory. When presented with a new piece of information during negotiations, write it down or draw it. When making an important point, write it down on a piece of paper before speaking. Do your calculations in detail in advance, because your sleep debt is going to get worse once negotiations start.

- Organize and simplify information as much as you can. Sleep deprivation impairs your ability to recollect and reproduce information. Consider this when compiling data and organizing information for negotiations. Do not keep vital information spread out across various platforms, such as e-mail, smartphone, files, folders, and notepads. Keep key information written down on a piece of paper.

- Beware of the decimal error. You would be amazed by how many brilliant and diligent minds have overlooked an incorrectly placed decimal point.

- Again, sleep on it! This enables the unconscious to work on the problems, and gives negotiators time to collect opinions before meeting again the next day. Anthropologist Clotaire Rapaille suggests that the transition between wakefulness and sleep allows a new kind of thinking, "...calming their brainwaves, getting them to that tranquil point just before sleep."

Summary: Alertness, Emotional Intelligence, Informational Intelligence

- Schedule the toughest negotiations around the most alert time (around eight in the morning in most cases.)
- Beware of a low PASS (Patel's Alertness Sleepiness Scale) during crucial parts of negotiations.
- Move around. Eat less. Avoid alcohol. Caffeine may help. Sit straight.
- Face the light. Minimize darkness. Keep the blinds up and lights on.
- Find out the emotional makeup of attendees in advance. Maintain eye contact as much as possible. Be perceptive. Recognize and manage emotions.
- Look for greater good when faced with ethical dilemmas.
- Look for collaboration, as opposed to conflict.
- Recognize waning motivation in your team as negotiations drag on.

- Humor can bring people together and advance the cause. It can break the ice. Use it appropriately.
- Write or, better yet, draw.
- Do not keep vital information stored across e-mail, smartphone, laptop, and notepads. Consolidate it in one location. Draw your BATNA on a piece of paper.
- Do not trust your memory when sleep deprived. Refer to your notes often.
- Protect interests more than methods.
- Beware of internal and external distractions. Maintain focus on the task at hand.
- Listen to the lazy one on the team.
- Speak slowly and clearly. Pause and smile. Look in others' eyes when speaking.
- Avoid trying the same unsuccessful method.

Leading from the Bag: Excelling Despite Jet Lag

In today's global economy, transcontinental mobility equals upward mobility. This section focuses on excelling even while traveling across multiple time zones. It begins with a brief description of the deficits caused by circadian misalignment and then gives practical tips to help you overcome these deficits so you can continue to excel, even on the road. These tips are arranged into three groups: before the trip, during the trip, and returning from the trip.

Suprachiasmatic Nucleus, Our Internal Clock

On the undersurface of our cerebral cortex, we have a tiny structure called the suprachiasmatic nucleus, our internal clock, which is responsible for the circadian rhythm present in numerous physiological functions. This internal clock manages daily fluctuations in alertness, sleepiness, mood, memory, hunger contractions, secretion of digestive juices, muscle tone, skin temperature, colon and bladder motility, blood pressure, and heart rate.

Rapid travel across multiple time zones causes misalignment of one's circadian rhythm with the external environmental rhythm, resulting in insomnia, daytime sleepiness, upset stomach, easy fatigability, irritability, and nervousness. Mood, motivation, goal setting, negotiation skills, communication, public speaking, strategy formulation, computation, data evaluation, and optimism are adversely affected.

Our preexisting sleep debt makes this problem worse. As we all have experienced, we do a lot of catching up prior to leaving the country, which leads to insufficient sleep. This sleep debt grows rapidly as we travel across multiple time zones. As discussed previously, this sleep deprivation adversely affects our executive center (prefrontal cortex) and fear center (amygdala). Combined with rhythm mismatch, this leads to severely suboptimal leadership while traveling. This fact is scary considering that in this age of globalization, leaders regularly make costly decisions while traveling across multiple time zones.

Excel at Three in the Morning?

Imagine giving a sales presentation to a key client at three in the morning while carrying an unusual amount of sleep debt. This is what you are doing when you give a presentation in London at eight in the morning (GMT) and your home zone is in the middle of the night. Can you be passionate while presenting? Can you maintain eye contact with key decision-makers? Can you gauge their mood and change the tone accordingly? Can you feel their pain? Can you connect? Can you maintain grace under fire? Can you quickly incorporate new information? Can you look for and find common ground? Can you look for the greater good? Can you close the deal?

In short, can you excel when leading from the bag? With proper planning and discipline, you certainly can. So let's start planning!

Before Taking the Trip

- Pay back as much sleep debt as you can by advanced planning and prioritization. Use the concept of sleep banking to your advantage, and try to get eight hours of sleep each night the week before a long trip. As difficult as it is, do everything possible to avoid late nights the week preceding the trip.

- Do not procrastinate when preparing for the trip. If you need an updated financial statement, ask for it as soon as you think about it. If you need to go over sales projections, go over them now. If your PowerPoint presentation is missing something, don't wait until you are on the plane to add it.

- Schedule smartly. If your first destination is London, your first night of sleep will begin about eleven o'clock local time, which is six in the evening your time, assuming you are from the East Coast. Try to go to bed a half hour or so earlier the week before. Also try to eat your meals an hour or so earlier for the same reason.

- Shift in advance. If you are traveling westward, postpone your sleep-wake and meal times by an hour or so the week prior to your trip. Remember, it is relatively easier to adapt to westward travel because it is easier to postpone than advance our sleep-wake schedule. Also, the fact that our circadian rhythm is slightly longer than twenty-four hours helps the realignment process during westward travel. Hence the saying, "West is the best!"

- Consider a sleeping pill. Sleep debt and circadian mismatch cause suboptimal leadership while traveling. You can easily treat sleep debt with a sleeping pill taken every other night or just on the night preceding a very demanding day. An ideal sleep aid should induce six to eight hours of sleep with a normal percentage of deep sleep, without causing tolerance or addiction. Discuss this with your family physician or, better yet, a sleep physician, well in advance of the trip. Try the pill at home first. Make sure it does not cause automatic behavior at night and sleepiness the next day. Take enough pills with you in your carry-on luggage.

- Recognize that business class is worth the added cost. If possible, travel business class, assuming you do not have a private jet or Air Force One. This is not because of physical inconvenience associated with the travel, but because of suboptimal leadership due to sleep disruption on long flights. The added cost of travel will pay handsome dividends in improved executive function and add value to your bottom line. But if you, as a rising entrepreneur or an employee of a firm going through financial hardship, are compelled to travel economy class, buy an inflatable bed, a first-class sleeper, from Amazon.com. With eight or ten breaths, this long pillow turns your coach seat into a bed—not a flat one of course—by supporting your head, neck, back, and buttocks. Try it. You may like it. If this does not work, avoid the red-eye flight if you can. Take pride in coach class. There is one very important thing to remember: do travel with pride and dignity. There is no shame in "simple living, high thinking." After being thrown out of a first-class coach on South African Railway in 1893 because of the color of his skin, Mahatma Gandhi always traveled third class. I always proudly tell my buddies that I travel "Gandhi Class," not coach class. Also remember that when traveling coach class, most of us are closer to our customers and constituents—a strategic advantage. Beware of a silent killer called economy-class syndrome: a blood clot that forms in the leg veins, travels to the lungs, and kills. Walk frequently. Maintain hydration. Avoid caffeine and alcohol, both of which dehydrate you. Drink water or juice. Do leg exercises, and ankle, knee, and hip movements, even while seated.

- Consider the tough challenges you will face when you return. There's one more scheduling consideration: if you are on a multiple-destination trip, then New York–Europe–Middle East–India–New York gives you the best leadership on the road. But if you need maximal alertness and leadership at home when you come back, then New York–India–Middle East–Europe–New York will make it easier for you to adjust and excel at home upon returning.

- Compile data in one location, as recommended earlier.[3] Travel adversely affects your working memory, information processing, creative problem solving, and data recollection. So have a detailed plan written or, better yet, drawn on one piece of paper for each meeting and each destination. Do not leave important information spread across several e-mails, multiple folders on your laptop, on your smartphone, and in several folders in your briefcase.

- Designating a deep thinker back home is more important than ever before. Remember, sleep deprivation adversely affects our executive center (prefrontal cortex) and our fear center (amygdala). This causes severe decline in your emotional and informational intelligence.

---

3 A few of the recommendations are repeated here as our global traveler may want to refer just to this section again prior to the trip.

How can you excel despite this handicap? You can team up with a trusted buddy who is staying back home. Your home-time buddy is not fighting circadian mismatch and sleep debt. This is analogous to assigning a designated driver. It can save you a fatal crash. Go over your goals and strategy for this trip with your buddy. Leave a copy of your plan with him or her. And when faced with a challenging situation while traveling, pick up the phone and consult your buddy back home. If it is not possible to have a buddy from your workplace for political or other reasons, you can designate your spouse, one of your parents, or your mentor to be your home-time buddy.

- Remember a few seemingly minor points: pack your own pillow, alarm clock, and Bible or other religious book. Your head, and perhaps your brain, will feel at home even in a hotel bed in Amsterdam with the feel of your own pillow. A small travel clock will alleviate anxiety over that six o'clock wake-up call for an eight o'clock meeting. Your brain would also love waking up to the same tune every morning. Also, carry your own copy of a religious book for regular reading. I have found that even a very brief reading unlocks that untapped spiritual force dormant within all of us. You will need this force even more when traveling, especially when faced with insurmountable obstacles or ridden with self-doubt.

- Recognize that the first day after landing is the worst. Your alertness, and hence your leadership, will be at its lowest on the first day after rapid travel through multiple zones. If possible, plan your presentation or negotiations on the second day of your arrival. Use the first day to gather local intelligence. Visit their manufacturing facility. Go to church or to a ball game with them the day before. Learn about their organizational culture—the actual culture practiced on the floor and not the one you read about on the company's website.

- Remember what a Harvard Business Review blog says, "You can't be CEO if you can't sleep on the plane."

In the movie Forrest Gump, Bubba, while leaning on Forrest's back at night in the dense and dark jungles of Vietnam during the war, said, "This way we don't have to sleep with our head in the mud."

A Few Helpful Tips for In-flight Insomnia

Some people can sleep on a plane; others can't. In most situations, it is a case of learned insomnia. After a couple of long, tiring red-eye flights, our subconscious mind has learned to dread sleeping on the plane. The whole experience of being in the plane reminds our subconscious mind of the unpleasant experience it had in the past, which makes falling asleep difficult. This conditioned reflex goes on and on, in a vicious cycle that never ends. To interrupt this cycle, you can learn self-relaxation or meditation, listen to relaxing music, or read a relaxing book. You can also try a sleeping pill after discussing this with your doctor or a behavior therapist; this may interrupt the reflex, generate confidence, form a new reflex, and break the habit. A giraffe sleeps standing, and you can, too!

Here are a few additional tips for overcoming in-flight insomnia:

- Look around. Everyone is sleeping, and you can, too.
- Wear loose-fitting clothes. Slip-ons are better than tight socks and shoes.
- Drink plenty of fluids to fight dehydration from dry air.

- Stretch your legs and your back before retiring to your seat.
- Use eyeshades and earplugs.
- Support your back, especially if you have a back problem.
- Use the power of visualization to your advantage. Imagine you are in your bed with your head on your pillow.
- Say a brief prayer before you go to sleep.
- Do not get restless and upset if you cannot sleep. Just relax.

When you feel discomfort while playing tennis or working on a project, you still keep going. Do the same thing while trying to sleep on the plane.

Sweet dreams!

During the Trip: Excelling Away from Home

A true leader has developed oneness with the universe and feels at home in Mumbai, Dubai, Budapest, and Beijing. As we discussed earlier, to excel on the road, you must go against the might of Mother Nature. You are fighting two tiny structures, the suprachiasmatic nucleus (your internal clock) and the amygdala (the fear center), and one not-so-tiny structure, your prefrontal cortex (the executive center). It will take discipline, devotion, faith, and perseverance to prevail and excel. In most cases, there will be tremendous financial motivation that can pull up your performance, but do remember that while motivation can improve attention, it cannot improve creativity and problem solving. Nor can motivation improve your ability to process, retain, digest, recollect, and apply relevant information for the greater good, and it cannot improve your social skills, your mood, or your optimism.

First things first: alcohol hurts executive function. Alcohol disrupts your deep sleep and makes your sleep nonrestorative. In short, it gives you insufficient and poor quality sleep! Alcohol does not mix at all with sleeping pills, either. So, if you are planning to take a sleeping pill on a flight to the Middle East, do not drink in the lounge or on the flight.

I know a drink is tempting, especially when it is complementary, but resist it. You will be making such tough choices all through the trip. Even a small amount of alcohol, when combined with sleep debt, will cause severe impairment in your leadership performance. You may miss a tremendous opportunity, overlook key financial information, or destroy a long-term amicable relationship with a colleague across the ocean.

So politely decline to drink, certainly during lunch and immediately before bedtime. Blame it on me. Say it's because of doctor's orders or health reasons. You can improvise. Offer a rain check, or say you really want Starbuck's or a Diet Coke. Maybe you will learn more about your colleague's negotiation style before that afternoon meeting.

In some places, it might be customary to drink during lunch hours, with beer in China, bitter beer with fish and chips in England, vodka in Russia, or wine in France. As appropriate, take a sip from someone else's drink; you can use the unused side of the glass. Or order a test dose, or take a bottle with you for the early evening enjoyment.

Understand that you are going against the might of Mother Nature. They are not. You are outnumbered and weak already. They have their entire upper management and all the company resources at their fingertips. You have a small team of sleep-deprived buddies. The general consensus in sleep medicine is that one should not consume alcohol within six hours of bedtime because it robs one of deep and restorative stages of sleep. I try to be nice to my patients and advise them to avoid it within three hours of bedtime. You can start drinking at five, stop at seven, and go to bed at ten. A perfect evening! You can drink, but at the right time, in the right amount, and with the right people. You should be doing this anyway, even at home.

Here are a few more recommendations that can help you excel on the road:

- If you have packed sleeping pills, take one at night to pay back your sleep debt. Use them based on your needs and as your physician advises.

- Stay active. Exercise every day, preferably in the morning. It will improve your alertness, clarify your thinking, and help your body adjust to the new rhythm. Do not exercise just before bedtime.

- Follow the LAMP (Leader's Alertness Maximization Plan).

- Avoid bright light in the evening, and sport those dark designer glasses. Seek sunlight in the morning because it will maximize alertness during the daytime.

- Do not forget your designated deep thinker. Keep in touch with him/her so he/she stays in the loop and is up to speed right away when you need advice.

- Set your smartphone screen to display dual time zones (home and local) so you know when you might be vulnerable and when you might be at your best. If it is one o'clock in the afternoon in New Delhi, it is two-thirty in the morning in New York. Now you know why your thinking is not quite clear and why your eyes are heavy. This is a perfect time to recharge with a PREM nap.

- Recognize that a perfectly timed ten- to fifteen-minute PREM nap can save your stakeholders a significant amount of wealth. It can improve your leadership performance for up to 150 minutes, according to several studies. What an investment! In some cultures, it might even be customary. Use it to your advantage. You can say, "Guys, I know we are pressed for time, but it is three o'clock in my hometown, and I could really use a fifteen-minute siesta. Could you guide me to a quiet place?" This is wisdom, not weakness.

- Avoid heavy meals during the entire trip. Small frequent snacks can maintain your energy without making you sleepy. A carbohydrate meal at dinner and a protein-rich meal (grilled/baked fish or chicken) at lunch are perfect. Avoid rice, pasta, bread, and dessert during lunch; you can savor them at dinnertime.
- Write, draw, and write some more. Take copious amounts of notes. They will come in handy on your return, because your ability to recollect information accurately is severely affected by jet-lag syndrome and sleep debt.
- Avoid renting a car. A sleep-deprived leader, unfamiliar neighborhood, and a mind preoccupied with executive challenges will lead to a fatal accident. The human race needs you badly. Stay alive. Avoid drowsy driving.

> "Winston is back," read the telegram from the Board of the Admiralty to the fleet when Winston Churchill was reinstated as army chief on September 3, 1939, the day Britain declared war on Germany.

Returning Home: A Smooth Landing

These tips will help you achieve a smooth landing on your return home:

- Perform routine catch-ups on the day you return, but wait until the second day and after to tackle tough tasks. Your alertness and your leadership are suboptimal on the first day of your return.
- Continue to follow the LAMP (Leader's Alertness Maximization Plan).

- Take sleeping pills as appropriate so you do not accumulate sleep debt.
- Be extra careful while driving, especially in the afternoon and on the first couple of days. The human race needs you to be alive.
- Avoid heavy meals and certainly avoid alcohol at lunchtime.
- Proudly take a PREM nap when sleepy. Enjoy coffee when naps are not feasible.
- Consider taking melatonin. There are no long-term safety studies available, but melatonin can shift your circadian rhythm if used at the correct time. When traveling, you do not stay at one location long enough to need realignment. Realignment is necessary on returning to your home time zone. Consult your physician. Only use a licensed, quality-controlled melatonin product at the lowest effective dosage. In most cases, it is recommended that you take melatonin an hour before your desired sleep time.
- Do not let your guard down, thinking, "I am home." Continue to strive for excellence and keep on looking for greater good.

There was a large study of 3,237 night-shift workers in Europe that showed significant cognitive slowing compared to their colleagues who were not exposed to circadian disruption.

I experienced this firsthand during my once-a-week thirty-six-hour call and once-a-month seventy-two-hour weekend call for sixteen years. Only after I stopped taking these night calls, on August 18, 2009, did I realize how truncated my leadership and, in fact, my life was. I began to notice a remarkable and rapid improvement in my leadership skills. I was thinking clearer. I was a better team player. I was not grumpy at work or at home. I could truly see a bigger picture. My long-term vision grew sharper, and my problem solving was amazingly effective.

Because of the negative effects of circadian-rhythm disruption, make major life and career decisions only after a weeklong lazy vacation, when your thinking is clearer, your emotions are positive, your outlook on life is broader, and your big-picture skills are sharper. Write them down in great detail, and refer to them periodically, because they will surely fade once you are back in the world of circadian disruption and sleep debt.

Travel and Conquer

President Obama flies to Europe for the G9 summit. He is sleep deprived at the beginning of the trip. Being a hands-on president, he is briefed in detail about the issues he will be discussing with other dignitaries attending the summit. He catches three to four hours of sleep en route in his bedroom on Air Force One, perhaps after a glass of wine. And he is meeting these leaders at nine o'clock GMT (three o'clock in the morning EST) to discuss, among other things, global recession and the stimulus package to jump-start the global economy.

Here is another scenario. Your vice-president of sales is taking his team to Dubai to secure a multimillion-dollar deal. He just got back this morning from Shanghai after closing a similar deal. He and his team have been busy going over the strategy for this coveted deal while drinking coffee all day long. In the evening, they get in the company jet and continue their discussion, but over several bottles of wine this time. Sleep deprived to start with, your vice-president catches six hours of sleep in the flat bed. Several members of your team keep on crunching the numbers for a long time and get only three hours of sleep. Their presentation starts at eight o'clock in the morning local time (one o'clock in the morning home time).

President Obama, your vice-president, and other members of their teams need their emotional intelligence and informational intelligence to be at their best. Their problem-solving skills, creativity, negotiations skills, social skills, and flexible decision making all need to be at their best. But they are not—because of suboptimal alertness due to preexisting sleep debt, which is making their jet-lag syndrome worse. Would you vote for Mr. Obama or any other candidate who goes drunk to such events? Being sleepy is no different. It may even be worse because the impairment is less obvious. Is it not in your interest to educate your vice-president and, in fact, all your employees on the importance of sleep? Would you pride yourself in hiring the eternally impaired people in your company?

Pilots, commercial truck drivers, and doctors-in-training have laws ensuring adequate sleep before they can report for work. Is your work less important? Should there be similar laws for leaders in private and public sectors? Should you include the importance of sleep in your company's mission, vision, and values? Would you want your colleagues to report to work leaving their brain on the pillow at home? Can an alert workforce give you competitive advantage over your competitor's drowsy workforce?

Female Leaders Are Unique

Female leaders are unique. Besides fighting male dominance on their ascent to the top, female leaders, while shouldering more than their share of family responsibilities, also have to fight insufficient deep sleep during premenstrual syndrome, menstruation, pregnancy, lactation, menopause, and even after menopause. If you add poor sleep hygiene to the list, what you get is severely suboptimal leadership. So it is of paramount importance that female leaders follow sleep hygiene with fervor and fanaticism.

We will describe several useful interventions that can help female leaders improve their sleep during these unique times. And, as always, learning about these deficits and being aware of them is half the battle.

Excelling Despite PMS and Menstruation

According to the National Sleep Foundation's women-and-sleep poll, half of menstruating women complain of disrupted sleep for three days during each menstrual cycle. For female leaders suffering from premenstrual syndrome, sleep disruption and the resultant drop in daytime alertness are even worse. Also, the hormone progesterone, which peaks during the second half of the menstrual cycle, exacerbates fatigue and excessive daytime sleepiness. These recurring challenges can take a toll on leadership and the life of our female leaders.

> The following tips can help. Remember that if you master these interventions, you get recurring return on your investment month after month throughout your career:

- Follow sleep hygiene with a fervor. Mother Nature is not helping you, so you will have to help yourself.
- Remember that exercise will help fight PMS symptoms and improve your REM sleep.
- Gradually taper off caffeine completely. Besides disrupting your deep sleep, caffeine contributes to premenstrual bloating.
- Drink more during the daytime. Drink plenty of fluids all day, but stop drinking in the evening to avoid nocturnal urination.
- Avoid the it-is-just-PMS attitude. Take your PMS seriously, and consult your physician to reduce PMS symptoms of bloating, breast

tenderness, back pain, cramping, irritability, nervousness, and grumpiness.

- Schedule lightly. You may argue that this is not always possible, but with proper planning, you might be able achieve this. Try to squeeze in a PREM nap in your busy schedule if you can.

- Do not let pride prevent you from seeking support. You know you are fighting Mother Nature, but no one else does because you cannot share this with your male colleagues. This should not prevent you from seeking support from your female colleagues and, for sure, your family members.

- Learn mindful meditation. It will help you deal with untoward emotions and will also treat that feeling of powerlessness that you, as a leader, hate.

Leading while Sleeping for Two

Pregnancy can severely affect the quality and quantity of your executive output because of poor sleep resulting from hormonal and other physiological changes your body goes through during pregnancy. According to the National Sleep Foundation's 1998 *women-and-sleep* poll, 78 percent of women reported more disturbed sleep during pregnancy than at other times. Following are the common problems responsible for disturbed sleep during pregnancy:

- **Insomnia.** Pregnant leaders may report difficulty falling asleep, staying asleep, waking up too early, or waking up tired. Stress or anxiety about labor, delivery, and motherhood may result in significant sleep loss. The discomforts of pregnancy, such as nausea, back pain, and fetal movements, may also disturb sleep.

- **Restless leg syndrome (RLS).** Symptoms of restless leg syndrome include unpleasant feelings in the legs, sometimes described as creepy, tingly, or achy. These feelings are worse at night or in the hours before bedtime. Movement or stretching temporarily relieves them. In a study of more than six hundred pregnant women, 26 percent reported symptoms of RLS.

- **Sleep apnea.** Hormonal changes relax your upper airway muscles, which may result in snoring and sleep apnea (repeated cessation of respirations lasting for ten or more seconds and robbing you of your deep sleep, causing severe daytime sleepiness and fatigue). Untreated, sleep apnea also increases the risk of gestational hypertension, preeclampsia, and low birth weight. Answer the following questions; if you reply yes to two or more, you are at high risk for obstructive sleep apnea and should talk to your doctor. A simple home sleep test can diagnose this serious disease. There is a safe, easy, and very effective treatment called continuous positive airway pressure (CPAP). CPAP hooks to a nasal mask or cannula, which acts as a pneumatic splint that keeps the airway open, thus eliminating snoring, sleep apnea, sleep disruption, and the apnea-related complications.

  S —Do you **snore** loudly?

  T— Do you often feel **tired**, fatigued, or sleepy during the daytime?

  O— Has anyone **observed** you stop breathing during sleep?

  P— Do you have or are you being treated for high blood **pressure**?

- **Nocturnal gastro-esophageal reflux (nighttime GERD).** Also known as heartburn, GERD is considered a normal part of pregnancy. However, nighttime symptoms of GERD can damage the esophagus and disrupt sleep during pregnancy. One study found that 30 percent to 50 percent of pregnant women experience GERD almost constantly during pregnancy.

- **Frequent nighttime urination.** The frequent need to urinate at night is a common feature of pregnancy and can result in loss of sleep.
- **Rising progesterone levels.** These exacerbate fatigue, tiredness, and excessive daytime sleepiness, especially in the first trimester.

Doctor's Orders

Sleeping well throughout pregnancy can be challenging. Follow these coping tips throughout your pregnancy to minimize loss of sleep:

- Plan, schedule, and prioritize sleep. Follow sleep hygiene with twice the fervor and fanaticism, as you are indeed sleeping for two.
- Avoid caffeine completely because it will compound the problem of insufficient deep sleep. Being a diuretic, caffeine will also increase your frequency of urination.
- After checking with your physician, exercise for at least thirty minutes per day.
- Sleep on your left side to improve the flow of blood and nutrients to your fetus and your uterus and kidneys. Keep your knees and hips bent. Place pillows between your knees, under your abdomen, and behind your back; this may take pressure off your lower back. Try to avoid lying on your back for extended periods of time. You may try special pregnancy pillows, which can help you be comfortable during sleep.
- Drink lots of fluids during the day, especially water, but cut down on the amount you drink in the hours before bedtime.
- If you can't get to sleep for twenty minutes, don't lie in bed and force yourself to sleep. Get out of the bedroom, and read a relaxing book, knit or crochet something for your baby, write in a journal, or take a warm bath.

- Learn progressive muscle relaxation. This will help your insomnia, and it will come in handy during delivery.

- Avoid looking at bright light at night. A nightlight in the bathroom will be less stimulating, allowing you to return to sleep more quickly.

- On work days, take a PREM power nap in the early afternoon. On weekends, you can take a longer nap in the afternoon to pay up your sleep debt. If you have difficulty falling asleep at night, then nap earlier in the day or curtail the duration of the nap.

- To avoid heartburn, do not eat large amounts of spicy, acidic, or fried foods. Also, eat frequent small meals throughout the day.

- Recognize that snoring is very common during pregnancy, but if you have pauses in your breathing associated with your snoring, you should be screened for sleep apnea.

- If you develop RLS, seek medical attention. Your doctor will check you for iron or folate deficiency.

- Keep your legs elevated at work and at home as much as you can. This can prevent leg swelling and may help your RLS. Leg-stretching exercises can help RLS, too.

God bless you both!

Leading During Menopause and Beyond

During the transition phase leading to menopause over several years, a woman's ovaries gradually decrease production of estrogen and progesterone. A woman reaches menopause one year after menstrual periods have stopped, usually around the age of fifty. Menopause is a time of major hormonal, physical, and psychological change. Natural changes in sleep also occur, characterized by longer time to sleep onset, frequent awakenings, decreased amount of deep sleep, and poor sleep architecture. From *perimeno-pause* to postmenopause, women report hot flashes, mood disorders, insomnia, and sleep-disordered breathing. Sleep problems are often accompanied by depression and anxiety, which make insomnia worse. This is the reason postmenopausal women are less satisfied with their sleep and why as many as 61 percent report insomnia symptoms. Snoring and sleep apnea have also been found to be more common and more severe in postmenopausal women because their upper airway dilator muscles become flabby with aging.

Changing and decreasing levels of estrogen cause many menopausal symptoms, including hot flashes, which are unexpected feelings of heat all over the body, accompanied by sweating. They usually begin around the face and spread to the chest, affecting 75 percent to 85 percent of women around menopause. On average, hot flashes last three minutes and lead to less sleep efficiency. Most women experience these for one year, but about 25 percent have hot flashes for five years. Hot flashes interrupt sleep and reduce the amount of deep sleep, leading to suboptimal alertness and suboptimal leadership the following day.

Talk to your doctor about estrogen (estrogen replacement therapy, or ERT) or estrogen and progesterone (hormone replacement therapy, or HRT), nutritional products, and medications such as calcium supplements, vitamin D, and bisphosphonates for the prevention or treatment of osteoporosis (thinning and weakening of the bones). Also discuss estrogen creams and rings for vaginal dryness, as well as alternative treatment for menopausal symptoms, such as soy products (tofu, soybeans, and soy milk), which contain phytoestrogen, a plant hormone similar to estrogen. Soy products may lessen hot flashes. Phytoestrogens are also available in over-the-counter nutritional supplements (ginseng, extract of red clover, and black cohosh). The FDA does not regulate these supplements. Their proper doses, safety, and long-term effects and risks are not yet known.

Typically, a leader's career spans five to six decades. And toward the later part of your career, because of your vast experience, a lifelong network of experts, and the wisdom that comes only with age, you are worth more than you ever were. This makes it imperative that you take good care of your sleep and your health so you can continue to contribute to the welfare of the human race; in other words, take your menopausal symptoms seriously and seek professional help.

Doctor's Orders

Here are a few tips to help you sleep well:

- Continue to follow sleep hygiene and insomnia instructions.

- Avoid foods that are spicy or acidic because these may trigger hot flashes. Try foods rich in soy because they might minimize hot flashes.

- Avoid nicotine, caffeine, and alcohol, especially before bedtime. These will make your hot flashes worse.

- Dress in lightweight clothes to improve sleep efficiency. Avoid heavy, insulating blankets, and consider using a fan or air-conditioner to cool the air and increase circulation. If your spouse is shivering, place a small portable heater next to his side of the bed. Manufacturers of the Sleep Number bed have come out with a mattress with separate temperature controls for you and your spouse.

- Reduce stress and worry as much as possible. Try relaxation techniques, massage, and exercise. Talk to a behavioral health professional if you are depressed, anxious, or having problems.

> • Try consolidating your sleep by going to bed thirty minutes later than your usual bedtime. As we age, we spend more time in bed, but sleep less.

Drowsy Driving Kills

About thirty-eight thousand people die on American roads each year. That is four preventable deaths every hour, mostly of people in their prime. By the time you finish reading this book, eight people will have died, and at least four of them as a result of drowsy driving, according to the National Highway Safety Administration.

On the very first day of my internship in this country, I did an initial evaluation of a female executive, who paramedics brought to the ER of Englewood Hospital Medical Center in Englewood, New Jersey. She was a restrained driver of a Volvo that ran off the road and into a tree on that cloudy afternoon on her way home to Englewood Cliffs from Newark Airport after a long transcontinental flight. Even though her car was totaled, she fortunately suffered only a minor chest contusion. What struck me, though, was her answer when I asked her what had happened. "I just don't know," she said.

That is the commonest answer I have heard during my twenty years of pulmonary practice while evaluating and treating survivors of motor-vehicle accidents. I was baffled with that answer until I started my sleep-medicine fellowship and learned about microsleeps and lack of situational awareness resulting from sleep deprivation. Microsleeps are fatal. Microsleeps, those ten to twenty seconds of sleep activity seen on electroencephalographic

(EEG), or brain wave, recordings of awake individuals, are uncontrollable sleep attacks occurring without any warning in patients with both acute and chronic sleep deprivation.

Loss of situational awareness kills, too. The other dangerous phenomenon seen in sleep-deprived leaders is the loss of situational awareness. With this deficit, the person loses awareness of his or her surroundings. Is the road ahead curving? Is there a reduced speed limit ahead? Is the car in the front braking? Are the driving conditions dangerous?

Beware of impaired decision-making too. When you are sleep deprived, your decision-making is so impaired that you may take a left turn when you should have waited. You may pass a truck on a curvy road, which you would not have done when rested. Or you may choose to text back while driving, which you would not have done if you were not sleep deprived.

Stay Awake, Drive Safe

A group of patients who had fallen asleep driving and survived to talk about it, along with our staff at the Indiana University Health Sleep Disorders Center in Goshen, started the "Stay Awake, Drive Safe" public awareness campaign in 2002. Its purpose is to eliminate drowsy driving by educating drivers about the dangers of drowsy driving and the countermeasures they can employ to survive. Please remember that turning on the radio, stretching your neck, putting a fan on high, putting your face out the window, slapping your face, or pushing a sharp pin in your thigh does not work. Following are the countermeasures that do work:

Doctor's Orders

- Certainly before a long trip, plan and get a good night's sleep.
- Avoid driving from midnight to six o'clock in the morning.
- Be extra careful while driving in the midafternoon.
- Do not drive after an overnight flight.
- Take a break at least every two to three hours.
- Take a PREM nap in anticipation of sleepiness.
- Remember that a cup of coffee can be lifesaving.
- If your thoughts become dreamy, your eyelids feel heavy, or traffic signs do not mean much, pull over: you are about to die!

Watchdogs Can't Be Sleepy

Journalists, the watchdogs of democracy, work long hours and get an insufficient amount of sleep. This can cause significant adverse effects to their alertness and their information-management skills, but they may not be aware of these deficits because of impaired self-evaluation due to an underactive prefrontal cortex (the executive enter). This is scary, especially considering that they have to analyze an enormous amount of information in a very short time. They have to broadcast this information in a comprehensible manner and sometimes without much rehearsal.

General Tips for Journalists

Use these tips to maximize your alertness and minimize the effects of sleep deprivation:

- Use the afternoon circadian dip in alertness to your advantage. Take a nap after lunch to pay up your sleep debt. Avoid an evening nap because it can disrupt your sleep.

- Exercise for thirty minutes every day. This will improve your deep sleep and your alertness, emotions, and information management. It may take some creative planning to fit this into your busy schedule. Pedal a stationary bike[4] while reviewing data, watching TV, or taking a break from work.

- Beware of bagginess. Sleep deprivation will make under-eye bagginess worse. Your makeup artist can help. But better yet, just sleep well—you will look and feel better, too!

- Talk slow and think fast. Cognitive slowing occurs with sleep deprivation. Avoid tongue twisters. Sleep deprivation affects verbal fluency. Short sentences are perfect.

- Compile data in one location. Write or, better yet, draw. Visual memory is less affected than verbal memory.

- Recognize that sleep deprivation forms false memory. Retrieval of information is impaired. Always check and recheck facts, especially when sleep deprived.

- Also, review and follow the recommendations for impaired informational intelligence discussed in Section III.

---

4 I call it "iPedal"

Tips for the Early Morning Media Person

The following tips will help the early morning media person excel despite insufficient sleep and circadian mismatch:

- Enjoy a good lunch. Avoid a starchy heavy dinner.
- On weekends, if you sleep in until eight or nine, truncate or even eliminate the afternoon nap. If you prefer to continue the weekday routine, that is perfectly fine, too.
- Avoid caffeine after one o'clock in the afternoon. Early morning caffeine will help maximize alertness, but use it judiciously.
- Stay alert while driving to work, especially on those dark winter mornings. Most fatal accidents occur during early morning hours.
- Avoid alcohol within three hours of bedtime because it will rob you of your REM sleep and make your sleep nonrestorative. Start drinking early!
- Avoid staring at bright light in the evening. It will make it harder to fall asleep at ten o'clock.

Tips for the Late Night Media Person

It is relatively easier for the late-night anchor because it is easier to postpone sleep than to advance it. This is, in part, because our sleep-wake cycle is slightly longer than twenty-four hours. The following recommendations will help you excel:

- Sleep from two o'clock to ten o'clock in the morning if you can. To help you sleep until ten o'clock, make sure your windows have dark drapes and the phone is turned off.
- Make sure your family members respect your sleeping through the morning hours. Put a "shift worker at sleep" sign on your bedroom door.

- If you can't sleep until ten, then catch up by napping for an hour or two after a good lunch. Make sure you take this catch-up nap as early as possible in the afternoon so it does not interfere with your sleep onset at night.

- Stay alert driving home after work, especially on those dark winter mornings. Most fatal accidents occur between midnight and six o'clock.

Happy reporting!

Concluding Comments

I suffered through ICU calls that were thirty-six hours and sometimes seventy-two hours long from 1989 to 2009. During that time my leadership and my life passed by, which I did not realize at the time. I have combined that unique experience with the latest medical research to come up with a framework that will empower you to regain that lost leadership and life itself. I want you to be better prepared than I was at handling crises both at home and at work, and more importantly, at enjoying work and cherishing this wonderful gift called life.

Remember that we are here on this beautiful earth for only a finite amount of time. The only way we can squeeze maximum life out of each moment is by maximizing our alertness, even during stressful periods. I know this is an uphill battle, but with patience, perseverance, practice, and faith, you will learn to excel and enjoy despite unavoidable sleep debt.

Guard your sleep like you guard your life. And when you cannot get sufficient sleep because of stress at home or at work, use the LAMP to maximize alertness. Leverage this alertness to maximize your emotional intelligence and informational intelligence. Add selflessness and spirituality to this mix, and you will maximize your God-given potential.

God Bless. Best Wishes. Keep in Touch.

Appendix A

Behavior change takes time, patience, and persistence. Follow me on twitter.com/yatinjpatel and receive my tweets about sleep disorders, sound sleep tips, sleep news, leadership, and life. Here are a few of my past tweets:

- Pleasant and perpetual perception is a prerequisite to consistent excellence.
- Sleep on your back and avoid facial wrinkles.
- As I dream 2night, my Lord, take me to enchanted corners of every galaxy.
- Dreams are a testament to brain's limitless imagination. Dream well 2night.
- As I sleep, my Lord, replace hatred from my subconscious with faith and love. Good night 2 all.
- Austerity of speech consists in speaking truthfully and beneficially & in avoiding offensive speech.
- Imagination is a virtue of REM sleep more than of wakefulness.
- REM sleep is the epicenter of innovation.
- Teens need 9 hrs sleep 2B happy, smart, & safe driver. It is 9 PM EST. Teens go 2 bed, Uncle Doc's order!
- Awake, I am in Goshen. Asleep, I am everywhere.
- Sleep is temporary death. And death is temporary sleep. Have a blast every moment.
- We are what we think. Let us have noble thoughts today. Great morning to all!

- Humor and happiness stabilize a leader's intellect.
- Even when sleepy, spread contagious enthusiasm & optimism across the organization.
- Do not dwell on unpleasant aspect of your work. REM sleep will magnify these negative emotions.
- Be the most educated and informed person in the industry by being a lifelong student.
- Accidents and poor decisions occur @ midafternoon. Drive alert. Sleep on a tough decision.
- Wakefulness is the way to life.
- Live a lifetime in each moment by pleasant and maximal alertness.
- As I sleep, Lord, fill up my vast subconscious with hope, happiness, joy, & bliss. And then wake me up with highest level of consciousness.
- Kill Monday morning blues today. Walk with a bounce, talk with a smile, and work with joy.
- Help me serve humanity with unshakable faith, empathy, and enthusiasm. Great morning to all.
- Do not fight Mother Nature. Maintain regular sleep wake schedule this weekend and avoid Monday morning blues.
- Truncated alertness leads to truncated life. Can infinite alertness lead to infinite life?
- Post lunch dip in alertness leads to disastrous mistakes. Avoid heavy lunch today. Plan a power nap. Keep moving. Face the light.
- Sleep is temporary death. Is death temporary sleep?

Appendix B

Patel's Alertness Sleepiness Scale Rating (PASS) (modified from Stanford Sleepiness Scale) to help you monitor your alertness at any given moment. Use it for sure to avoid task-ability mismatch:

Feeling active, vital, alert, or wide awake	10
Functioning at high levels, but not at peak Able to concentrate	8
Awake, but relaxed Responsive, but not fully alert	6
Somewhat foggy Letdown	4
Foggy Losing interest in remaining awake Slowed down	2
Sleepy, woozy, or fighting sleep Prefer to lie down	0

Epworth Sleepiness Scale (ESS) determines the level of sleepiness you are experiencing because of cumulative sleep debt. ESS is a measure of chronic (long-term) sleepiness, while Patel's Alertness Sleepiness Scale (PASS) is a measure of your sleepiness at a given moment. To get your ESS, use the following scale to choose the most appropriate number for each situation:

0   would never doze or sleep

1   slight chance of dozing or sleeping

2   moderate chance of dozing or sleeping

3   high chance of dozing or sleeping

Situation	Chance of Dozing or Sleeping
Sitting and reading	
Watching TV	
Sitting inactive in a public place	
Being a passenger in a motor vehicle for an hour or more	
Lying down in the afternoon	
Sitting and talking to someone	
Sitting quietly after lunch (no alcohol)	
Stopped for a few minutes in traffic while driving	
Total:	

If you add up the total score, this is your ESS score. A score of ten or more is considered sleepy. A score of eighteen or more is very sleepy. If you score ten or more on this test, you should consider whether you are obtaining adequate sleep, need to improve your sleep hygiene, and/or need to see a sleep specialist.

Sleep Hygiene Score

How can you measure and then monitor your sleep hygiene? Here is a simple quiz designed for that purpose:

- Do you get at least eight hours of sleep every night with a regular sleep-wake schedule, even on weekends?

- Do you use the bedroom only for sleep and sex?

- Do you avoid alcohol within three hours of bedtime and caffeine after one o'clock?

- Do you exercise at least twenty minutes a day?

- Do you pray before you go to bed?

Give yourself two points for each favorable answer. In order to earn maximum return on your investment in sleep, you have to score ten on the sleep hygiene measure.

Alertness Intelligence Quiz

Acquiring alertness intelligence is the first step to becoming an AEI∞ leader.

- Have you been sleeping well for seven to eight hours for the past week?

- Did you sleep well for seven to eight hours last night?

- Are you feeling maximally alert right now?

- Can you sustain maximal alertness all day?

- Did you exercise for twenty minutes or more today?

Give yourself two points for each yes answer and zero points for each no answer. The first question checks whether you are not carrying sleep debt; the second one, whether you are suffering from acute sleep deprivation. The third and fourth questions determine whether your alertness is maximal and sustainable. The last one measures your practice of sleep hygiene.

Emotional Intelligence Quiz for Sleep-Deprived Leaders

If you answer these five simple questions, you will know your emotional intelligence score:

- Can you recognize your emotions?

- Can you manage your emotions?

- Can you recognize others' emotions?

- Can you manage others' emotions?

- Are your social skills at their best?

Give yourself two points for each yes answer and zero points for each no answer. The first two questions measure self-awareness and interpersonal awareness. The next one measures interpersonal intelligence, which the last two questions measure your social skills. Ten out of ten is a perfect score.

Informational Intelligence Quiz

- Can you receive information accurately?

- Can you process it effectively?

- Can you apply it appropriately?

- Are you the most informed person in the company?

- Are you the best speaker in the company?

Give yourself two points for each yes answer and zero points for each no answer. The first four questions measure your ability to acquire, process, and apply information to the task at hand. The last one measures your commitment to continuing education.

Selflessness Quiz

- Do you follow the 80/20 rule for selfless thinking?

- Do you follow the 80/20 rule for selfless speech?

- Do you follow the 80/20 rule for selfless action?

- Do you spend two hours a week doing charity work?

- Are you in contact with a selfless mentor?

Give yourself two points for each yes answer and zero points for each no answer. Ten out of ten is a perfect score.

Spirituality Quiz

- Do you pray before starting your day?

- Do you pray before retiring to bed?

- Do you use a one-line prayer during your work?

- Do you go to a spiritual retreat every six months?

- Are you in contact with a spiritual guru?

Give yourself two points for each yes answer and zero points for each no answer. Ten is a perfect score.

Appendix C

Leader's Alertness Maximization Plan (LAMP)
when faced with sleep deprivation:

- Keep moving.
- Face the light.
- Take a PREM nap.
- Get a relaxing massage.
- Snack smartly.
- Consume caffeine judiciously.
- Seek spiritual support.
- Avoid alcohol.

Emotionally intelligent leadership even when sleep deprived:

- Exude contagious enthusiasm and optimism. It will spread rapidly across the organization.

- Recognize that a smile is your savior. Humor and happiness stabilize a leader's intellect. Smile often. Stay close to people with a positive demeanor.

- Recognize that pause is your partner. Pause before answering. Save emotional e-mails in the drafts folder and send them the next morning. If it is a complicated issue or a vital one, sleep on it.

- Do not dwell on the unpleasant aspect of your work.

- Pray often. When on the go, read a line from the Bible or other spiritual book.

- Replace fear and anger with faith and empathy through mental discipline.

- Avoid irritability. Take a walk, talk to your spouse, nap, meditate, exercise, and play. Beware of delicate situations that can exaggerate irritability. Tactfully avoid them or live through them quietly.

- Listen to the lazy one on your team or in your life.

- Look for collaboration and creativity.

- Set the goals high.

Informational intelligence even when sleepy:

- Solicit novel ideas and suggestions. Methods should be flexible; goals may not be.

- Avoid internal distractions. Train your mind to stay focused on the task at hand. One pointed mind will achieve more at a majestic pace than a distracted mind at a frantic pace.

- Minimize external distractions. Discourage your colleagues from making distracting comments. Politely bring them back to the task at hand.

- Compile vital information in one location as opposed to keeping it in various folders in various locations.

- Write, draw, write, draw, and remember. Verbal memory is more affected than visual memory.

- Prepare, write, and rehearse. Speak slowly and clearly. Avoid tongue twisters and long sentences.

- Scrutinize, verify, and dissect the data. At retrieval, sleep deprivation causes false memories.

- Seek simplicity. Bravely and mercilessly weed out unnecessary detail.

- Sleep on it if possible. REM sleep causes crazy creativity. Or listen to the lazy one in your team, or consult your spouse, your parents, your mentor, or your well-rested buddy.

- Do not try failed solutions repeatedly.

Ten Steps to AEImax

1. Follow sleep hygiene with fervor.

2. Develop alertness awareness. Throughout the day and at critical moments, use PASS to rate your alertness.

3. With practice and persistence, eliminate preventable causes of sleep deprivation.

4. Expertly use countermeasures to neutralize midafternoon grogginess and jet-lag inefficiency.

5. Use PREM naps routinely to maximize your alertness and your leadership.

6. Continue to develop your emotional intelligence with particular focus on empathy.[1]

7. Be pleasantly aware of your emotional intelligence throughout the day, definitely during the critical moments.

8. Learn to manage information effectively with special focus on distilling information for greater good.

9. Be the most educated and informed person in the industry by being a lifelong student. Continuing education is infinitely more important than conventional education because it is more relevant and more pertinent to the task at hand. By focusing on continuing education, dropouts like Steve Jobs and Bill Gates excelled in their industry. Mahatma Gandhi said, "Live as if you were to die tomorrow; learn as if you were to live forever."

10. Practice and improve your listening and public speaking skills. Be the best listener and speaker in the industry.

---

1 I found Daniel Goleman's book, *Emotional Intelligence*, immensely useful. You can also attend seminars to improve your emotional intelligence. Or you can hire an executive coach who specializes in emotional intelligence training.

Seven Steps to AEI∞ Leadership

- Disciplined personal finances will help your journey toward selflessness.

- Solicit your spouse and children's cooperation in your quest for greater good.

- Look for common interests and actions that can help both you personally and the organization. Slowly advance this process as you follow the 80/20 rule of selflessness. Think, speak, and act 80 percent of the time for the greater good and 20 percent of the time for your immediate family.

- Mentor with a leader in the industry who has devoted his whole life selflessly to a noble cause.

- Make a conscious effort to encourage selflessness in your colleagues. This will then help you in your own journey toward selflessness.[31]

- Choose a spiritual guru, and keep in close contact. Attend a spiritual retreat every six months. Buddha said, "Be in company of the wise, or better yet live with them."

- Develop a daily prayer routine. Pray in the morning and at bedtime. When you are extremely busy and on the go all the time, you may not have enough time for a complete prayer, but a line or two on the go will suffice. "Come, Holy Spirit" is what Father Theodore Hesburgh recites religiously when he wakes up, before he retires to bed, and several times during the day. Such practice will recharge your spiritual engine and allow you to tap into that unending source of energy.

---

2 When he was engineering the company's turnaround in 2008, Howard Shultz, the founder and CEO of Starbuck's, took ten thousand store managers, against the advice of his management team, to New Orleans to volunteer. He later opined, "If we wouldn't have had New Orleans, we wouldn't have turned the company around."

Appendix D

Suggested Books

The Harvard Medical School Guide to a Good Night's Sleep (Harvard Medical School Guides) by Lawrence Epstein and Steven Mardon (paperback)

The Promise of Sleep: A Pioneer in Sleep Medicine Explores the Vital Connection Between Health, Happiness, and a Good Night's Sleep by William C. Dement and Christopher Vaughan (paperback, 2000)

Emotional Intelligence: 10th Anniversary Edition; Why It Can Matter More Than IQ by Daniel Goleman

Say Good Night to Insomnia by Gregg D. Jacobs (paperback, 2009)

The Insomnia Workbook: A Comprehensive Guide to Getting the Sleep You Need by Stephanie Silberman and Charles Morin (paperback, 2009)

No More Sleepless Nights by Peter Hauri and Shirley Linde (paperback, 1996)

Restful Insomnia: How to Get the Benefits of Sleep Even When You Can't by Sondra Kornblatt and Teresa E. Jacobs, MD (paperback, 2010)

I Can Make You Sleep: Overcome Insomnia Forever and Get the Best Rest of Your Life! by Paul McKenna (hardcover and CD, 2009)

Cognitive Behavioral Treatment of Insomnia: A Session-by-Session Guide by Michael L. Perlis, Carla Jungquist, Michael T. Smith, and Donn Posner (paperback, 2008)

Power Sleep : The Revolutionary Program That Prepares Your Mind for Peak Performance by James B. Maas, Megan L. Wherry, David J. Axelrod, and Barbara R. Hogan (paperback, 1998)

Take a Nap! Change Your Life by Sara Mednick and Mark Ehrman (paperback, 2006)

Permission to Nap: Taking Time to Restore Your Spirit by Jill Murphy Long (paperback, 2002)

Sleep to be Sexy, Smart, and Slim by Ellen Michaud (hardcover, 2008)

A Woman's Guide to Sleep: Guaranteed Solutions for a Good Night's Rest by Joyce Walsleben and Rita Baron-Faust (paperback, 2001)

Sleep Deprived No More: From Pregnancy to Early Motherhood—Helping You and Your Baby Sleep Through the Night by Jodi A. Mindell (paperback, 2007)

The Well-Rested Woman: 60 Soothing Suggestions for Getting a Good Night's Sleep by Janet Kinosian (paperback, 2002)

Suggested Websites

http://www.sleepfoundation.org/

National Sleep Foundation

http://www.nhlbi.nih.gov/about/ncsdr/

National Center on Sleep Disorder Research, National Institute of Health

http://www.circadian.com/

CIRCADIAN® provides consulting, training, technology, and information to solve the challenges of the 24/7 workforce.

http://www.alertness-solutions.com/

Alertness Solutions provides innovative and effective solutions that enhance safety, performance, and health in diverse settings.

Suggested Review Articles with Detailed Bibliography

"Understanding the Effects of Sleep Deprivation on Executive Function, Complex Task Performance, and Situation Awareness," by Nancy Lynn Grugle, dissertation submitted to the Faculty of the Virginia Polytechnic Institute and State University, March 14, 2005, Blacksburg, Virginia

"Sleep Deprivation: Impact on Cognitive Performance" by Paula Alhola, Päivi Polo Kontola Department of Psychology, Sleep Research Unit (Department of Physiology), University of Turku, Turku, Finland

"Sleep Loss and Sleepiness" by Thomas J. Balkin, PhD, Tracy Rupp, PhD, Dante Picchioni, PhD, and Nancy J. Wesensten, PhD. *CHEST* / 134 / 3 / September 2008, www.chestjournal.org

Appendix E

Bibliography

Sleep deprivation and alertness

Akerstedt, T., Gillberg, M. 1990. Subjective and objective sleepiness in the active individual. *Int J Neurosci* 52:29–37

Balkin, T. J., Reichardt, R., and Wesensten, N. J. 2005. Chronic sleep restriction and resatiation: II. Recovery of subjective alertness [abstract] *Sleep* 28(suppl):O398.

Carskadon, M. A., and Dement, W. C. 1979. Effects of total sleep loss on sleep tendency. *Percept Mot Skills* 48:495–506.

Casagrande, M., Violani, C., Curcio, G., et al. 1997. Assessing vigilance through a brief pencil and paper letter cancellation task (LCT): Effects of one night of sleep deprivation and of the time of day. *Ergonomics* 40:613–30.

Dement, W. C., Carskadon, M. A., and Richardson, G. 1978. Excessive day-time sleepiness in the sleep apnea syndrome. In: Guilleminault, C., Dement, W. C., eds. Sleep apnea syndromes. New York, NY: Liss. 23–46.

Johns, M. W. 1991. A new method for measuring sleepiness: the Epworth Sleepiness Scale. *Sleep* 6:540–545.

McKenna, J. T., Tartar, J. L., Ward, C. P., et al. 2007. Sleep fragmentation elevates behavioral, electrographic and neurochemical measures of sleepiness. *Neuroscience* 146:1462–1473.

Porkka-Heiskanen, T., Strecker, R. E., Thakkar, M., et al. 1997. Adenosine: a mediator of the sleep-inducing effects of prolonged wakefulness. *Science* 276:1265–1268.

Wesensten, N. J., Killgore, W. D., Balkin, T. J. 2005. Performance and alertness effects of caffeine, dextroamphetamine, and modafinil during sleep deprivation. *J Sleep Res* 14:255–266.

Sleep deprivation and emotional intelligence

Brendel, D. H., Reynolds, C. F. III, Jennings, J. R., et al. 1990. Sleep stage physiology, mood, and vigilance responses to total sleep deprivation in healthy 80-year-olds and 20-year-olds. *Psychophysiology* 27:677–85.

Dinges, D. F., Pack, F., Williams, K., et al. 1997. Cumulative sleepiness, mood disturbance, and psychomotor vigilance performance decrements during a week of sleep restricted to 4–5 hours per night. Sleep 20: 267–277.

Drummond, S. P., Paulus, M. P., Tapert, S. F. 2006. Effects of two nights sleep deprivation and two nights recovery sleep on response inhibition. *J Sleep Res* 15:261–5.

Horne, J. A. 1993. Human sleep, sleep loss and behaviour implications for the prefrontal cortex and psychiatric disorder. *Br J Psychiatry* 162:413–9.

Kalin, N. H., Shelton, S. E., 2004. The role of the central nucleus of the amygdala in mediating fear and anxiety in the primate. *Journal of Neuroscience* 24(24):5506–15.

Killgore, W. D., McBride, S. A., Killgore, D. B., et al. 2006. The effects of caffeine, dextroamphetamine, and modafinil on humor appreciation during sleep deprivation. *Sleep* 29:841–847.

Mikulincer, M., Babkoff, H., Caspy, T., et al. 1989. The effects of 72 hours of sleep loss on psychological variables. *Br J Psychol* 80 (Pt 2):145–62.

Richards, J. M., Killgore, D. B., Killgore, W. D. 2006. The effect of 44 hours of sleep deprivation on mood using the Visual Analog Mood Scales [abstract]. *Sleep* 29(suppl):A132–A133.

Sagaspe, P., Sanchez-Ortuno, M., Charles, A., et al. 2006. Effects of sleep deprivation on color-word, emotional, and specific stroop interference and on self-reported anxiety. *Brain Cogn* 60:76–87

Van der Helm, E., Gujar, N., Walker, M. P. 2010. Sleep deprivation impairs the accurate recognition of human emotions. Sleep and Neuroimaging Laboratory, Department of Psychology, University of California, Berkeley. *Sleep* 33(3):281–2.

Van Dongen, H. P., Maislin, G., Mullington, J. M., et al. 2003. The cumulative cost of additional wakefulness: dose-response effects on neurobehavioral functions and sleep physiology from chronic sleep restriction and total sleep deprivation. *Sleep* 2003.

Van Dongen, H. P., Baynard, M. D., Maislin, G., et al 2004. Systematic interindividual differences in neurobehavioral impairment from sleep loss: Evidence of trait-like differential vulnerability. *Sleep* 27:423–33.

Sleep deprivation and information intelligence

Babkoff, H., Zukerman, G., Fostick, L., et al. 2005. Effect of the diurnal rhythm and 24 h of sleep deprivation on dichotic temporal order judgment. *J Sleep Res* 14:7–15.

Baddeley, A. D., Hitch, G. J. 1974. Working memory. *Academic Press*. p. 47–89.

Baranski, J. V., Pigeau, R. A., Angus, R. G. 1994. On the ability to self-monitor cognitive performance during sleep deprivation: A calibration study. *J Sleep Res* 3:36–44.

Baranski, J. V., Pigeau, R. A., 1997. Self-monitoring cognitive performance during sleep deprivation: Effects of modafi nil, d-amphetamine and placebo. *J Sleep Res* 6:84–91.

Belenky, G., Wesensten, N. J. , Thorne, D. R., et al. 2003. Patterns of performance degradation and restoration during sleep restriction and subsequent recovery: A sleep dose-response study. *J Sleep Res* 12:1–12.

Binks, P. G., Waters, W. F., Hurry, M. 1999. Short-term total sleep deprivations does not selectively impair higher cortical functioning. *Sleep* 22:328–34.

Blagrove, M., Alexander, C., Horne, J.A. 1995. The effects of chronic sleep reduction on the performance of cognitive tasks sensitive to sleep deprivation. *App Cogn Psych*, 9:21–40.

Casement, M. D., Broussard, J. L., Mullington, J.M., et al. 2006. The contribution of sleep to improvements in working memory scanning speed: A study of prolonged sleep restriction. *Biol Psychol* 72:208–12.

Chee, M. W., Chuah, L. Y., Venkatraman,V., et al. 2006. Functional imaging of working memory following normal sleep and after 24 and 35 h of sleep deprivation: Correlations of fronto-parietal activation with performance. *Neuroimage* 31:419–28.

Chee, M. W., Choo, W. C. 2004. Functional imaging of working memory after 24 hr of total sleep deprivation. *J Neurosci* 24:4560–7.

Choo, W. C., Lee, W. W., Venkatraman, V., et al. 2005. Dissociation of cortical regions modulated by both working memory load and sleep deprivation and by sleep deprivation alone. *Neuroimage* 25:579–87.

Dinges, D.F., Kribbs, N. B. Performing while sleepy: effects of experimentally-induced sleepiness. In: Monk TH, ed. *Sleep, sleepiness and performance.* New York, NY: John Wiley and Sons, 1991; 97–128.

Doran, S. M., Van Dongen, H. P., Dinges, D. F. 2001. Sustained attention performance during sleep deprivation: Evidence of state instability. *Arch Ital Biol*, 139:253–67.

Engleman, H. M., Kingshott, R. N., Martin, S. E., et al. 2000. Cognitive function in the sleep apnea/hypopnea syndrome (SAHS). *Sleep* 23(suppl):S102–S108.

Harrison, Y., Horne, J. A. 1999. One Night of sleep loss impairs innovative thinking and flexible decision making. *Organ Behav Hum Decis Process* 78:128–145.

Horne, J. A. 1988. Sleep loss and "divergent" thinking ability. *Sleep* 11:528–536.

Verstraeten, E. Neurocognitive effects of obstructive sleep apnea syndrome. 2007. *Curr Neurol Neurosci Rep* 7:161–166.

Wilkinson, R. T., Edwards, R. S., Haines, E. 1966. Performance following a night of reduced sleep. *Psychon Sci* 5:471–472.

Sleep deprivation and AEI leadership

Belenky, G., Wesensten, N. J., Thorne, D. R., et al. 2003. Patterns of performance degradation and restoration during sleep restriction and subsequent recovery: a sleep dose-response study. *J Sleep Res* 12:1–12.

Durmer, J. S., Dinges, D. F. 2005. Neurocognitive consequences of sleep deprivation. *Semin Neurol* 25:117–129.

Gillberg, M., Kecklaund, G., Akerstedt, T. 1994. Relations between performance and subjective ratings of sleepiness during a night awake. *Sleep* 17:236–241.

Harrison, Y., Horne, J. A. 1999. One night of sleep loss impairs innovative thinking and flexible decision making. *Organ Behav Hum Decis Process* 78:128–45.

Hsieh, S., Li, T. H., Tsai, L. L. 2010. Impact of monetary incentives on cognitive performance and error monitoring following sleep deprivation. Cognitive Electrophysiology Laboratory, Department of Psychology & Institute of Cognitive Science, National Cheng Kung University, Tainan, Taiwan, ROC. *Sleep* 33(4):499-507.

Kahn-Green, E. T., Day, L. M., Conrad, A. K., et al. 2006. Short-term vs. long-term planning abilities: differential effects of stimulants on executive function in sleep deprived individuals [abstract]. *Sleep* 29(suppl): A370.

Kamdar, B. B., Kaplan, K. A., Kezirian, E. J., Dement, W. C. 2004. The impact of extended sleep on daytime alertness, vigilance, and mood. *Sleep Med* 5(5):441–8.

Killgore, W. D., Balkin, T. J. , Wesensten, N. J. 2006. Impaired decision making following 49 h of sleep deprivation. *J Sleep Res* 15:7–13.

Killgore, W. D., Killgore, D. B., Killgore, Day, L. M., et al. 2007. The effects of 53 hours of sleep deprivation on moral judgment. *Sleep* 30: 345–352.

Linde, L., Bergstrom, M. 1992. The effect of one night without sleep on problem-solving and immediate recall. *Psychol Res* 54:127–36.

McKenna, B. S., Dicjinson, D. L., Orff, H. J., et al. 2007. The effects of one night of sleep deprivation on known-risk and ambiguous-risk decisions. *J Sleep Res*

Monk, T. H., Carrier, J. 1997. Speed of mental processing in the middle of the night. *Sleep* 20:399–401.

Nilsson, J. P., Soderstrom, M., Karlsson, A. U., et al. 2005. Less effective executive functioning after one night's sleep deprivation. *J Sleep Res*, 14:1–6. Ogawa, Y., Kanbayashi, T., Saito, .Y, et al 2003.

Rupp, T. L., Reichardt, R., Wesensten, N. J., et al. 2008. Sleep extension improves alertness and performance during and following 7 nights of subsequent sleep restriction [abstract]. *Sleep* 31(suppl):0325

Rupp, T. L., Raphael, A., Wesensten, N. J., et al. 2008. Prior sleep extension facilitates learning of a mathematical processing task during sleep restriction and recovery [abstract]. *Sleep* 31(suppl):0358.

Thomas, M., Sing, H., Belenky, G., et al. 2000. Neural basis of alertness and cognitive performance impairments during sleepiness: I. Effects of 24 h of sleep deprivation on waking human regional brain activity: *J Sleep Res* 9:335–352.

Tsai, L. L., Young, H. Y., Hsieh, S., et al. 2005. Impairment of error monitoring following sleep deprivation. *Sleep* 28:707–13.

Wimmer, F., Hoffmann, R. F., Bonato, R. A., et al. 1992. The effects of sleep deprivation on divergent thinking and attention processes. *J Sleep Res* 1:223–30

Dangers of drowsy driving

Otmani, S., Pebayle, T., Roge, J., et al. 2005. Effect of driving duration and partial sleep deprivation on subsequent alertness and performance of car drivers. *Physiol Behav*, 84:715–24.

Powell, N. B., Schechtman, K. B., Riley, R. W., et al. 2001. The road to danger: the comparative risks of driving while sleepy. *Laryn-goscope* 111:887–893.

Thorne, D. R., Thomas, M. L., Sing, H. C., et al. 1999. Driving-simulator accident rates before, during and after one week of restricted nightly sleep. *Sleep* 21:S135.

Sleep of female leaders

Alhola, P., Tallus, M., Kylmälä, M., et al. 2005. Sleep deprivation, cognitive performance, and hormone therapy in postmenopausal women. *Menopause* 12:149–55.

Dzaja, A., Arber, S., Hislop, J., et al. 2005. Women's sleep in health and disease. *J Psychiatr Res* 39:55–76.

Kalleinen, N., Polo, O., Himanen, S. L., et al. 2006. Sleep deprivation and hormone therapy in postmenopausal women. *Sleep Med* 7:436–47.

Stenuit, P., Kerkhofs, M. 2005. Age modulates the effects of sleep restriction in women. *Sleep* 28:1284–8.

Wright, K. P. Jr., Badia, P. 1999. Effects of menstrual cycle phase and oral contraceptives on alertness, cognitive performance, and circadian rhythms during sleep deprivation. *Behav Brain Res* 103:185–94.

Miscellaneous articles

Ayas, N. T., White, D. P., Al-Delaimy, W. K., et al. 2004. A prospective study of self-reported sleep duration and incident diabetes in women. *Diabetes Care* 27:282–284.

Banks, S., Van Dongen, H., Dinges, D. 2007. Can a night of sleep debt be recovered with one night of sleep [abstract]? *Sleep* 30(suppl):P0654.

Bonnet, M. H., Rosa, R. R. 1987. Sleep and performance in young adults and older normals and insomniacs during acute sleep loss and recovery. *Biol Psychol* 25:153–72.

Chaput, J. P., Despres, J. P., Bouchard, C., et al. 2008. The association between sleep duration and weight gain in adults: a 6-year prospective study from the Quebec family study. *Sleep* 31:517–523.

Carskadon, M. A., Dement, W. C. 2005. *Normal human sleep: An overview.* Philadelphia: Elsevier Saunders. p. 13–23.

Dorrian, .J, Rogers, N. L., Dinges, D. F. 2005. *Psychomotor vigilance performance: Neurocognitive assay sensitive to sleep loss.* New York: Marcel Dekker. p. 39–70.

Drummond, S. P., Brown, G. G. 2001. The effects of total sleep deprivation on cerebral responses to cognitive performance. *Neuropsychopharmacology* 25:S68–73.

Drummond, S. P., Brown, G. G., Gillin, J. C., et al. 2000. Altered brain response to verbal learning following sleep deprivation. *Nature,* 403:655–7.

Drummond, S. P., Brown, G. G., Salamat, J. S., et al. 2004. Increasing task difficulty facilitates the cerebral compensatory response to total sleep deprivation. *Sleep* 27:445–51.

Drummond, S. P., Brown, G. G., Stricker, J. L., et al. 1999. Sleep deprivation-induced reduction in cortical functional response to serial subtraction. *Neuroreport*, 10:3745–8.

Drummond, S. P., Gillin, J. C., Brown, G. G. 2001. Increased cerebral response during a divided attention task following sleep deprivation. *J Sleep Res* 10:85–92.

Durmer, J. S., Dinges, D. F. 2005. Neurocognitive consequences of sleep deprivation. *Semin Neurol* 25:117–29.

Ferrie, J. E., Shipley, M. J., Cappuccio, F. P., et al. 2007. A prospective study of change in sleep duration: associations with mortality in the Whitehall-II cohort. *Sleep* 30:1659–1666.

Forest, G., Godbout, R. 2000. Effects of sleep deprivation on performance and EEG spectral analysis in young adults. *Brain Cogn*, 43:195–200.

Frey, D. J, Badia, P., Wright, K. P. Jr. 2004. Inter- and intra-individual variability in performance near the circadian nadir during sleep deprivation. *J Sleep Res* 13:305–15.

Gosselin, A., De Koninck, J., Campbell, K. B. 2005. Total sleep deprivation and novelty processing: Implications for frontal lobe functioning. *Clin Neurophysiol*, 116:211–22.

Graw, P., Krauchi, K., Knoblauch, V., et al. 2004. Circadian and wake-dependent modulation of fastest and slowest reaction times during the psychomotor vigilance task. *Physiol Behav*, 80:695–701.

Habeck, C., Rakitin, B. C., Moeller, J., et al. 2004. An event-related fMRI study of the neurobehavioral impact of sleep deprivation on performance of a delayed-match-to-sample task. *Brain Res Cogn Brain Res* 18:306–21.

Harrison, Y., Espelid, E. 2004. Loss of negative priming following sleep deprivation. *Q J Exp Psychol A* 57:437–46.

Harrison, Y., Horne, J.A. 2000. Sleep loss and temporal memory. *Q J Exp Psychol A* 53:271–9.

Harrison, Y., Horne, J.A. 1998. Sleep loss impairs short and novel language tasks having a prefrontal focus. *J Sleep Res* 7:95–100.

Harrison, Y., Horne, J.A., Rothwell, A. 2000. Prefrontal neuropsychological effects of sleep deprivation in young adults–a model for healthy aging? *Sleep* 23:1067–73.

Heuer, H., Klein, W. 2003. One night of total sleep deprivation impairs implicit learning in the serial reaction task, but not the behavioral expression of knowledge. *Neuropsychology* 17:507–16.

Heuer, H., Kleinsorge, T., Klein, W., et al. 2004. Total sleep deprivation increases the costs of shifting between simple cognitive tasks. *Acta Psychol* (Amst) 117:29–64.

Heuer, H., Kohlisch, O., Klein, W. 2005. The effects of total sleep deprivation on the generation of random sequences of key-presses, numbers and nouns. *Q J Exp Psychol Appl* 58:275–307.

Heuer, H., Spijkers, W., Kiesswetter, E., et al. 1998. Effects of sleep loss, time of day, and extended mental work on implicit and explicit learning of sequences. *J Exp Psychol Appl* 4:139–62.

Horne, J. A., Pettitt, A. N. 1985. High incentive effects on vigilance performance during 72 hours of total sleep deprivation. *Acta Psychol* (Amst) 58:123–39.

Hublin, C., Partinen, M., Koskenvuo, M., et al. 2007. Sleep and mortality: a population-based 22-year follow-up study. *Sleep* 30:1245–1253.

Jennings, J. R., Monk, T. H., van der Molen, M.W. 2003. Sleep deprivation influences some but not all processes of supervisory attention. *Psychol Sci* 14:473–9.

Johnsen, B. H., Laberg, J. C., Eid, J., et al. 2002. Dichotic listening and sleep deprivation: Vigilance effects. *Scand J Psychol* 43:413–17.

Kendall, A. P., Kautz, M. A., Russo, M. B., et al. 2006. Effects of sleep deprivation on lateral visual attention. *Int J Neurosci* 116:1125–38.

Kilduff, T. S., Kushida, C. A., Terao, A. 2005. *Recovery from sleep deprivation.* New York: Marcel Dekker. p. 485–502.

Kim, D. J., Lee, H. P., Kim, M. S., et al. 2001. The effect of total sleep deprivation on cognitive functions in normal adult male subjects. *Int J Neurosci* 109:127–37.

Kjellberg, A. 1977. Sleep deprivation and some aspects of performance. II. lapses and other attentional effects. *Waking Sleeping* 1:145–8.

Kripke, D. F., Garfinkel, L., Wingard, D. L., et al. 2002. Mortality associated with sleep duration and insomnia. *Arch Gen Psychiatry* 59:131–6.

Knutson, K. L., Spiegel, K., Penev, P., et al. 2007. The metabolic consequences of sleep deprivation. *Sleep Med Rev* 11:163–178.

Lac, G., Chamoux, A. 2003. Elevated salivary cortisol levels as a result of sleep deprivation in a shift worker. *Occup Med* (Lond) 53:143–5.

Lee, H. J., Kim, L., Suh, K. Y. 2003. Cognitive deterioration and changes of P300 during total sleep deprivation. *Psychiatry Clin Neurosci* 57:490–6.

Linde, L., Edland, A., Bergström, M. 1999. Auditory attention and multi-attribute decision-making during a 33 h sleep-deprivation period: Mean performance and between-subject dispersions. *Ergonomics* 42:696–713.

Maquet, P. 2001. The role of sleep in learning and memory. *Science* 294:1048–52.

McCarthy, M. E., Waters, W. F. 1997. Decreased attentional responsivity during sleep deprivation: Orienting response latency, amplitude, and habituation. *Sleep* 20:115–23.

Mu, Q., Nahas, Z., Johnson, K. A., et al. 2005. Decreased cortical response to verbal working memory following sleep deprivation. *Sleep* 28:55–67.

Murillo-Rodriguez, E., Blanco-Centurion, C., Gerashchenko, D., et al. 2004. The diurnal rhythm of adenosine levels in the basal forebrain of young and old rats. *Neuroscience* 123:361–70.

Naghavi, H. R., Nyberg, L. 2005. Common fronto-parietal activity in attention, memory, and consciousness: Shared demands on integration? *Conscious Cogn* 14:390–425.

National Sleep Foundation. 2007. "Sleep in America" www.sleepfoundation.org.

Philibert, I. 2005. Sleep loss and performance in residents and nonphysicians; a meta-analytic examination. *Sleep* 28:1393–402.

Philip, P., Taillard, J., Sagaspe, P., et al. 2004. Age, performance and sleep deprivation. *J Sleep Res* 13:105–10.

Pilcher, J. J., Huffcutt, A. I. 1996. Effects of sleep deprivation on performance: A meta-analysis. *Sleep* 19:318–26.

Portas, C. M., Rees, G., Howseman, A. M., et al. 1998. A specific role for the thalamus in mediating the interaction of attention and arousal in humans. *J Neurosci* 18:8979–89.

Priest, B., Brichard, C., Aubert, G., et al. 2001. Microsleep during a simplified maintenance of wakefulness test. A validation study of the OSLER test. *Am J Respir Crit Care Med* 163:1619–25.

Quigley, N., Green, J. F., Morgan, D., et al. 2000. The effect of sleep deprivation on memory and psychomotor function in healthy volunteers. *Hum Psychopharmacol* 15:171–7.

Ragland, J. D., Coleman, A. R., Gur, R. C., et al. 2000. Sex differences in brain-behavior relationships between verbal episodic memory and resting regional cerebral blood flow. *Neuropsychologia* 38:451–61.

Raidy, D. J., Scharff, L. F. 2005. Effects of sleep deprivation on auditory and visual memory tasks. *Percept Mot Skills* 101:451–67.

Rinkenauer, G., Osman, A., Ulrich, R., et al. 2004. On the locus of speed-accuracy trade-off in reaction time: Inferences from the lateralized readiness potential. *J Exp Psychol Gen* 133:261–82.

Russo, M. B., Kendall, A. P., Johnson, D. E., et al. 2005. Visual perception, psychomotor performance, and complex motor performance during an overnight air refueling simulated flight. *Aviat Space Environ Med* 76:C92–103.

Samkoff, J. S., Jacques, C. H. 1991. A review of studies concerning effects of sleep deprivation and fatigue on residents' performance. *Acad Med* 66:687–93.

Sarter, M., Gehring, W. J., Kozak, R. 2006. More attention must be paid: The neurobiology of attentional effort. *Brain Res Brain Res Rev* 51:145–60.

Scoville, W. B., Milner, B. 2000. Loss of recent memory after bilateral hippo-campal lesions. 1957. *J Neuropsychiatry Clin Neurosci* 12:103–13.

Shneerson, J. M. 2000. *Handbook of sleep medicine*. Cambridge: Blackwell Science, 2000.

Smith, M. E., McEvoy, L. K., Gevins, A. 2002. The impact of moderate sleep loss on neurophysiologic signals during working-memory task performance. *Sleep* 25:784–94.

Smulders, F. T., Kenemans, J. L., Jonkman, L. M., et al. 1997. The effects of sleep loss on task performance and the electroencephalogram in young and elderly subjects. *Biol Psychol*, 45:217–39.

Spiegel, K., Leproult, M., L'Hermite-Baleriaux, et al. 2004. Leptin levels are dependent on sleep duration: relationships with sympathovagal balance, carbohydrate regulation, cortisol, and thyrotropin. *J Clin Endocrinol Metab* 89:5762–5771.

Spiegel, K., Knutson, K., Leproult, R., et al. 2005. Sleep loss: A novel risk factor for insulin resistance and type 2 diabetes. *J Appl Physiol*, 99: 2008–19.

Spiegel, K., Leproult, M., Van Cauter, E. 1999. Impact of sleep debt on metabolic and endocrine function. *Lancet* 354: 1435–1439.

Steyvers, F. J. 1987. The influence of sleep deprivation and knowledge of results on perceptual encoding. *Acta Psychol* (Amst) 66:173–87.

Stickgold R. 2005. Sleep-dependent memory consolidation. Nature, 437:1272–8.

Strangman, G., Thompson, J. H., Strauss, M. M., et al. 2005. Functional brain imaging of a complex navigation task following one night of total sleep deprivation: A preliminary study. *J Sleep Res* 14:369–75.

Swann, C. E., Yelland, G. W., Redman, J. R., et al. 2006. Chronic partial sleep loss increases the facilitatory role of a masked prime in a word recognition task. *J Sleep Res* 15:23–9.

Taillard, J., Moore, N., Claustrat, B., et al. 2006. Nocturnal sustained attention during sleep deprivation can be predicted by specific periods of subjective daytime alertness in normal young humans. *J Sleep Res* 15:41–5.

Thomas, M., Sing, H., Belenky, G., et al. 2000. Neural basis of alertness and cognitive performance impairments during sleepiness. I. effects of 24 h of sleep deprivation on waking human regional brain activity. *J Sleep Res*, 9:335–52.

Tomporowski, P. D., Tinsley, V. F. 1996. Effects of memory demand and motivation on sustained attention in young and older adults. *Am J Psychol* 109:187–204.

Van Dongen, H. P., Vitellaro, K. M., Dinges, D. F. 2005. Individual differences in adult human sleep and wakefulness: Leitmotif for a research agenda. *Sleep* 28:479–96.

Versace, F., Cavallero, C., De Min Tona, G., et al. 2006. Effects of sleep reduction on spatial attention. *Biol Psychol* 71:248–55.

Wilkinson, R. T. 1990. Response-stimulus interval in choice serial reaction time: Interaction with sleep deprivation, choice, and practice. *Q J Exp Psychol A* 42:401–23.

About the Author

Yatin J. Patel, MD, MBA, did his internal medicine residency (1989–1992) at Mount Sinai Hospital in New York, where he was also the chief resident. After finishing his pulmonary and sleep-medicine fellowship in 1994, he founded the Center for Sleep Studies and started his pulmonary and sleep-medicine practice at Indiana University Medical Center in Goshen, Indiana. He also serves as director of pulmonary medicine at the Center for Cancer Care. He is a senior fellow at the American College of Chest Physicians and American Academy of Sleep Medicine, where he is an active member of the sleep deprivation subcommittee.

In 2002, he started the public awareness campaign "Stay Awake, Drive Safe," aimed at eliminating drowsy driving-related accidents through educational events at schools, colleges, and highway rest plazas.

In 2008, he graduated magna cum laude from the Executive MBA Program, Mendoza College of Business, at the University of Notre Dame. Soon after graduation, he founded AEI Center for Supreme Leadership to promote selfless leadership focused on advancement of the human race.

His consulting firm, Alertonics, consults with organizations of various sizes, educates their executives on the importance of sleep, and helps sleep-deprived executives excel despite insufficient sleep. He conducts seminars, "Supreme Leadership through Sound Sleep" and "AEI∞ model of Supreme Leadership." He also teaches a course titled, "Sleep Well, Lead Well" to the executive MBA students at the University of Notre Dame.

He is a frequent contributor on WNDU (NBC), WSTV (FOX), WNIT (PBS), and B100 (radio), promoting sleep. His hobbies include nature, meditation, philosophy, wine, and cooking. He lives in Goshen, Indiana, with his wife, Dipti, his daughters, Priyata and Pooja, and his son, Parth.

Price: 15 USD

Profits from the sale of this book and from my consulting work will go toward establishing and supporting a global initiative, the F.E.M.A.L.E. (Food, Education, Medicines, And Love for Everyone) Ashram, aimed at changing the world by educating one neuron at a time through innovative intervention using the Internet and other media.

Made in the USA
Lexington, KY
25 September 2012